"GARDEN BOOK OF ....
2001   B.A.I.P.A.

" AWARD OF MERIT "
WRITER'S DIGEST

"The Book of Bromeliads"
and Hawaiian Tropical Flowers

Your Bromeliad Guide to Interiorscaping, Landscaping, Cut Flowers, and Live Floral Arrangements
Especially for Hotels, Shopping Centers, Condominiums, Professional Offices, Restaurants, Landscape Architects, Gardeners,
Collectors, Garden Centers, Nurseries, Landscapers, Interiorscapers, Home Owners and Florists

1999 Ronald W. Parkhurst

Lead Photographer	Iolanda Marquardt
Contributing Photographers	Ron Parkhurst, Randy Hufford, Chris Krumrey, Waterson Photography, Jacob & Mary Ann Doane Mau
Cover Photos, Front & Back	Photography thru Hawaiian Eyes, Jacob & Mary Anne Doane-Mau©
Ink Drawings	Sherette Shiigi
Billy the Bromeliad Illustration	Florence L. Parkhurst
Book Layout	Jim Frey
First Edition	March 2000 ISBN: 1-56647-326-8 5,000 copies
Jacket	Guzmania Super Puna Gold Cover
Jacket Design	Jim Frey / Ron Parkhust
Publisher	Pacific Isle Publishing Company P O Box 827 Makawao, HI 96768
Distribution	Pacific Isle Publishing Company P O Box 827 Makawao, HI 96768
Grown on Maui_{tm} Logo	Maui Flower Growers Association
Printed in	Taiwan

Library of Congress Catalog Number 00-104739

Disclaimer   Because of the possible unanticipated changes in governing statutes and case law relating to the application of any information contained in this book, the author, publisher, and any and all persons or entities involved in any way in the preparation, publication, sale, or distribution of this book disclaim all responsibility for the legal effects or consequences of any document prepared or action taken in reliance upon information contained in this book. No representations, either express or implied, are made or given regarding the legal consequences of the use of any information contained in this book. Purchasers and persons intending to use this book for the preparation of any legal documents are advised to check specifically on the current applicable laws in any jurisdiction in which they intend the documents to be effective.

By: Ronald W. Parkhurst
- Hanalei Nursery - Bromeliad Growers -

ink drawing by: Sherlette Shiigi

Bromeliads - The most diverse plant in the plant kingdom.

Credits

Since the word "The Book" is used on the front cover, we want to give recognition to the Father – Jehovah God, the Son – Jesus Christ, the Spirit – Holy Ghost.

To my wife Patrice, my daughter Elizabeth, my mother, our families, extended families, friends, spiritual mentors, kupuna's and all others.

In memory of Ben, Harry, Pearce, Priscilla, Priscilla, Richard, Richard, Betsy, Hugh, Ellen, Walter, Geoffrery (Howard Yamamoto who passed away while writing this book. Hawaii's premiere Bromeliad hybridizer and our mentor.)

To the Bromeliad Lovers who helped so much, Ted Umbour, Tom Lockard, David Shiigi, Howard Yamamoto, Tsuro Murakami, Baks, Duke Brown, Sharon Peterson, Rob Deleon, Geoffrey Johnson, Tony Godfrey, Luc Pieters, Betty Ho, Leiland Mylano, Bob Harvey, Alex Didio, Guy Haywood, Ron Gonzales and Christopher Krumrey.

Special thanks to Iolanda Marquardt, Jim and Val Frey, and Tom Grimston who without their help, this project would of remained an idea.

photo: Iolanda Marquardt

Ron Parkhurst

photo: Iolanda Marquardt

David Shiigi

Contents

Neoregelia - 'Scarlet Charlotte'

photo: Iolanda Marquardt

INTRODUCTION

There are many reasons for this book. First, this is your guide to Bromeliads, as a consumer, we hope to provide the "who", "what", "where, "when", and "why" of Bromeliads. A place where you can get general information and picture identifications. You will soon come to find that Bromeliads are the plant of the nineties and twenty first century.

What makes Bromeliads the most sought after plant for interior designs, landscaping, cut flowers and live floral arrangements? They are long lasting, have beautiful (inflorescence) flowers , attractive foliage, hundreds of varieties and are easy to care for. They are for novices and experts alike.

I hope that we can spark a flame for your interest in bromeliads. Since a picture is worth a thousand words, this book will be mostly pictures with a few words. This book will be your guide to "Bromeliads".

Billy the Bromeliad says: "How do you know when you are a bromeliad enthusiast? When it starts to <u>grow</u> on you!"

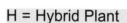

H = Hybrid Plant

S = Specie Plant

C = Collector Plant (rare)

T = Tissue Culture Plant or Commercial Plant

Guzmania 'Kapoho Flame'

photo: Idlanda Marquardt

HISTORY

Chapter 1

Bromeliads (bro-mee'-lee-ad's) belong to a specific plant family, Bromeliaceae, which encompasses approximately 3000 species and hundreds of hybrids, are native to the America's except one specie. The one exception, is found in Africa (there is a thinking that even this specie came from the Americas long ago).

Bromeliads are one of the larger plant families horticulturally and one of the most diverse families in the plant kingdom. Bromeliads are seed plants and do not reproduce by spores. These seeds are enclosed in an ovary (not a conifer) or "angiosperm". It is monocotyledon or one leaf on the sprout. The leaves have parallel veins. The flowers have petals, which are all alike, thus, identification can be the flowers, and parallel veined leaves with scales. The latter is what distinguishes bromeliads, which is very unique. This scale, which is called trichomes, allows the leaf to collect water.

The southern United States have many native Bromeliads and are protected by conservation laws. Spanish moss or "peles hair" is the oldest known bromeliad and found indigenous to the southern United States. The pineapple is the only edible bromeliad.

In nature, many bromeliads grow on trees or rocks as epiphytes or air plants. Their roots are used mainly for support and they are not parasites. Other bromeliads grow as terrestrials, growing in the ground and getting nutrients from their roots. Bromeliads are remarkably versatile and form one of the most adaptable plant families in the world. They are easy to grow and have many varieties, shapes and color combinations. Bromeliads can be broken down into three large subfamilies: a) Bromelioideae b) Pitcairnioideae c) Tillandsioideae. From there, Bromeliads are divided into groups called Genera, fifty-two total. The majority of the plants in each genus (singular for genera) have the same cultural requirements; there are exceptions of course. Different genera require varying amounts of light, water, air movement and temperature. The most common genera in cultivation are a) Aechmea, b) Billbergia, c) Cryptanthus, d) Guzmania, e) Neoregelia, f) Nidularium, g) Tillandsia, and h) Vriesea.

Bromeliads are the first choice in flowering plants for interiorscaping. They are also very popular in "accenting" landscape designs. Bromeliads have become the plant of the nineties and the twenty-first century. Some of the reason being that the flowers and foliage last a long time, require little care, are drought resistant, and are very hardy.

Billy the Bromeliad says:
History is Thistory.

Neoregelia Hybrids

Neoregelia Hybrid

Commercial, Collector and Hybrid Bromeliads

Chapter 2

A COMMERCIAL plant is grown in mass numbers to supply the markets. It is usually grown in a nursery that has greenhouses and benches with a controlled environment;

-meaning it could control defused light with shade cloth, usually between 50% and 80% shade.

-have temperature control by using heaters if necessary during winter months.

-proper air movement, such as with fans.

-having a watering system that also could inject fertilizers and pesticides.

A small greenhouse nursery business would be considered around 15,000-sq. ft. under roof and a large greenhouse nursery would be 30 acres or more under roof. This type of nursery operation will buy bromeliad seedlings from a tissue culture laboratory, that will mass produce thousands of plants from a single parent plant. This is one of the main reasons why the commercial plant is fairly inexpensive to buy at a wholesale price level of approximately $4.00 for a 4" potted flowering plant, $8.00 for a 6" potted plant, and $12.00 for a gallon potted flowering plant. Of course prices will vary depending on the plant, availability and market demand. It is interesting to note that varigated leaved plants (plants with white stripes down the center of green leaves) and albomarginata plants (plants with white borders on leaves and green down the center) can be reproduced in the lab, but the plant will not be consistent in the markings, so reproduction of these desirable plants are done by off shoots at the base of the mother plant. These varigated and albomargnata plants command a more premium price, because they cannot be mass-produced successfully in numbers in the lab.

COLLECTOR plants are the harder to find plants that are not being reproduced in the lab and are limited in numbers. It could be specie or a hybrid plant. What makes this plant desirable? All I can say is, "beauty is in the eyes of the beholder". This plant could be rare, have beautiful foliage or an unusual bloom. This is the bromeliad that will end up in a personal collection. Prices will vary on this plant greatly. Starting at a few dollars and going as high as a thousand dollars plus. Usually the collector plant will be under $50.00.

The HYBRID plant is a plant that has been cross-pollinated by two different parents. Usually the hybrid is kept within the plant genus, though inter-generic hybrids can be very popular. Sometimes when you cross-pollinate, the seedlings will be consistantly the same and mature in a like manner. Or you may only get one plant in ten thousand that is desirable. The time invested in seeing your new hybrid plant come into maturity from pollination is approximately 3 to 5 years, with some families taking longer. There are two different types of hybridizers, the hobbyist and the commercial breeder. One does it for the love of the plant; the other does it for love of the plant and financial success. Once a hybrid plant has been determined to have commercial potential, the hybridizer will seek to protect the hybrid with a plant patent. Patents or plant protection include European protection (10 nations), Japan protection, U.S. patents and others. It would be uneconomical to pull a world patent because of costs. Once a hybridizer has protected his plant, he will then seek a tissue culture lab to mass-produce the hybrid for the world markets. So again, the rule of thumb is that if a hybridizer develops a plant that is not mass-produced, the cost of the hybrid plant will be more expensive. On the other hand, a commercial hybridizer who can have his plant mass-produced, will be less expensive. Again, supply and demand.

Billy the bromeliad says: What's red, white and green all over? A neoregelia tri-color perfecta in bloom!

Guzmania 'Puna Gold'

photo: Iolanda Marquardt

11

Growing and Care of Bromeliads

Chapter 3

As many bromeliad growers there are in the world, you will have as many "mixatologists" that have there own way of growing bromeliads. There is nothing wrong with this. I will outline some of the basic growing and care tips that have proven successful for Hanalei Nursery – Bromeliad Growers. If you are getting liners from a tissue culture laboratory, you will want to transplant your plant in an intermediary pot. We use 2" pots, 49 per tray with a basic transplanting mix such as Sunshine One. We will sometimes use in our mix a time release fertilizer, such as 14-12-14 and a wetting agent. We will keep these plants in their pots until they are ready to transplant into their final pot, in approximately 6 months. From there we will make a new mix which will consist of 1/3 Sunshine One, 1/3 coarse peat, 1/3 sponge rock and 1/10 Vermiculite. We will then take the final pot and fill with 1/3 finish mix, from there we will add time release fertilizer, ½ tbl. For 4" pot, ¾ tbl. For 6" pot and 1 tbl for gallon pot. It is then mixed in the pot and more mix being added to the top of the pot. The plant is then taken out of the 2" pot and cleaned of the existing mix and planted 1" above the start of the root system. The soilless mix is then packed to 1" below the pot top and "watered in". Plants with new mix are then put on the bench.

The other method of transplanting is from an offshoot of the mother plant. First you must wait until the offshoot comes to mature size. This is usually 2/3 the size of the mother plant, minimal. Once you have an offshoot ready for removal, first see if you can remove it by wiggling it side to side and back and forth. If this does not work, take a serrated knife and cut vertically between the off shoot and the mother plant. After removal, let the offshoot sit for 24 hours to "dry out" the breakage. Then dip the end in a powdered rooting hormone, such as Hormex, found at your local garden store. Plant it in the appropriate sized pot, following the same instructions as above.

A basic rule of thumb for watering will be different in each area. It is good to let the plant dry out in the cup and also let the mix "start" to dry out before watering. If the cup or center of plant does not dry out, it is a good idea to flush out the cup with fresh water at least once a month (do not over water, bromeliads can rot!). They also like their foliage to be misted.

Beside the time release fertilizer I use in my pots, I like to use foliar fertilizer, such as Peters 20-20-20 at least once or twice a month. Never during their flowering cycle.

Most bromeliads like indirect light, though some can tolerate full sun. Air movement is also very important for healthy plants. Bromeliads will only bloom once. The average time of growth to a bloom is approximately 20 to 24 months. Another interesting factor with bromeliads is being able to induce a plant to bloom with certain types of chemicals. Bromeliads natural bloom cycle in Hawaii is spring and summer, in the other months we use an ethelene solution to induce blooming. Once a mature plant is forced to bloom, it will take approximately 8 to 14 weeks to reach a mature bloom. A slice of apple placed in the cup of the bromeliad, covered with cellophane will also cause the plant to bloom. This practice of forcing the plant to bloom was first discovered in Europe back in the early 1900's. Europe is credited with being the first region to grow and study bromeliads outside of their natural habitat. Their only disadvantage being their cold winter climate, which brings us back to our story. Because of this climate, greenhouses had to be constructed and heated during the winter months. At one time during some repair, some acetylene and oxygen spilled from the torches into the bromeliads during work, it was then observed that the plants in the area of work all bloomed within a certain time frame. To this day Europe still uses acetylene and water to induce blooming.

Billy the Bromeliad says:
T.L.C.F.B. Tender loving care for bromeliads.

Guzmania 'Maui Sunset'

photo: Iolanda Marquardt

Disease and Pests of Bromeliads

Chapter 4

The main pests in Hawaii for Bromeliads are scale, mealy bug, white fly, aphids and burrowing nematodes. Your local garden store can help you find the right product for your pest. We like to use products that are environmentally safe and using the stronger products only if necessary. We spray only if we see an infestation to prevent the pest from building up any resistance. IT IS ALSO INTERESTING TO NOTE HOW LIVE BROMELIADS CAN CONTRIBUTE TO CLEAN AIR IN A CLOSED ENVIROMENT SUCH AS BUILDINGS. THEY WILL TAKE TOXINS AND CO_2 OUT OF THE AIR AND PUT OXYGEN BACK IN! IT IS VERY HEALTH CONSCIOUS TO HAVE LIVE BROMELIADS IN YOUR ENCLOSED ENVIROMENTS.

Another disease that could effect your bromeliads is fungus. Again consult your local garden center to use the safest product available that will control this disease. At Hanalei Nursery, we have been experimenting with organic methods of controling pests and fungus, we use a combination of Dr. Bronner's peppermint soap and pine-sol. We mix 3 tablespoons each in a quart spayer, then fill with water. It is safe, smells good and you can work with your plants after spraying. It also helps control tree frogs.

The other factor that may have an effect on your bromeliad is a virus. To determine if your plant has a virus or another plant problem, you will have to take your plant to a specialist. On Maui, we are fortunate to have the University of Hawaii, Extension Service, which assists us in identifying disease and pests. Another source for identifying pests may be found in the private sector, State Department of Agriculture and the United States Department of Agriculture. One of these agencies will be able to direct you in the right direction. Make sure you isolate your diseased plants and remain so until the plant can be put back on the shelf. If your plant is not getting better, but worse, though this may be painful, destroy the plant to prevent further spreading of disease.

The last item I would like to discuss here is certification of your nursery plants. If you are at all considering selling your products to the public, it is important to consider certifying your nursery with the State Department of Agriculture. This will help prevent the spreading of alien species and pests from one area to another. You will be required to abide by certain specifications, sanitation and monthy reports. Though somewhat cumbersome, the positives out weigh the negatives.

Another good source of information about growing bromeliads is other bromeliad growers. We strongly recommend you support your local nursery association or a similar group, your local bromeliad society and Bromeliad Society International . The Internet is also a good source of information. Check out our homepage at http://maui.net/~hanalei/flower/

Billy the Bromeliad says: What's a bromeliad bug? No it's not a bromeliad pest, but more likely it could be a pesty bromeliad enthusiast!

14

Aechmea
'Little Harv'

photo: Iolanda Marquardt

AECHMEA

Chapter 5

The most popular bromeliad, besides the pineapple, is Aechmea Fasciata, thanks to the Europeans. It has been in cultivation since the early 1800's. It has a beautiful pink inflorescence and blue/purple flowers. This is an excellent plant to grow for the beginner or commercial grower. It is a hardy plant that does well. A lot of the Aechmea's unfortunately have thorns and one has to be careful not to get poked. Thanks to the DeLeon's and others, they have been on the lookout for thornless mutants. DeLeon is responsible for patenting the first thornless fasciata and has continued to improve their thornless varieties. Another popular Aechmea is the thornless Fancini or Friederike, which was patented in Europe.

Aechmea's not only have a long lasting inflorescence, but many varieties have very attractive foliage. Many Aechmea's can tolerate full sun, while other's require a shaded enviroment. The shapes are various and include vase like, bottle and tubular forms. The size also varies from very small (few inches) to over three feet in height! Foliage coloration ranges from maroons, pinks, reds, silvers, and greens with markings such as bands, marbles, variegated and albomarginata.

Billy the Bromeliad says: What do you call a sore bromeliad grower?Ache-me-ahhhh!!!!

Aechmea
lueddemanniana cv. 'Rodco'

photo: Ron Parkhurst

16

photo: Iolanda Marquardt

Aechmea - fosteriana
Species -x   *Collector -x*
Size: **24" high**   *Foliage Length:* **6 months**
1 gallen pot

photo: Iolanda Marquardt

Aechmea - orlandiana cv.'Black Beauty'
Hybrid -x   *Collector -x*
Size: **16" high**   *Flower Length:* **60 days**
Hybridizer: **Baensch 6" pot**

photo: Iolanda Marquardt

Aechmea - fulgens variegata
Species -x   *Collector -x*
Size: **12" high**   *Flower Length:* **30 days**
6" pot

photo: Iolanda Marquardt

Aechmea - chantinii
Species -x   *Collector -x*
Size: **20" high**   *Flower Length:* **45 days**
1 gallon pot

Aechmea -fasciata varigata

Species *-x*   **Commercial** *-x*
Size: 16" high   **Flower Length:** 60 days
1 gallon pot

Aechmea -fasciata Flower

Species *-x*   **Commercial** *-x*
Size: 24" high   **Flower Length:** 60 days
1 gallon pot

Aechmea - weilbachii

Species *-x*   **Collector** *-x*
Size: 16" high   **Flower Length:** 15 days
1 gallen pot

Aechmea - orlandiana

Species *-x*   **Collector** *-x*
Size: 16" high   **Flower Length:** 60 days
1 gallon pot

photo: Iolanda Marquardt

Aechmea - 'Little Harv'

Hybrid *-x*   **Commercial** *-x*
Size: **36" high**   *Flower Length:* **90 days**
Hybridizer: **Harvey Bullis**   **2 gallon pot**

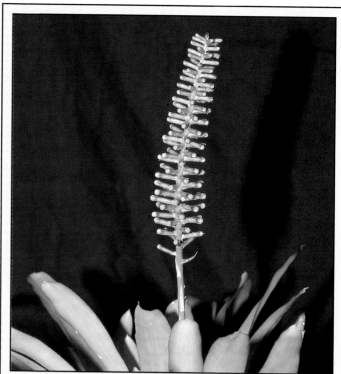

photo: Iolanda Marquardt

Aechmea - gamosepala

Species *-x*   **Collector** *-x*
Size: **14" high**   *Flower Length:* **15 days**
4" pot

photo: Iolanda Marquardt

Aechmea - 'Romero'
(thorn + thornless varieties)
Hybrid *-x*   **Commercial** *-x*
Size: **30" high**   *Flower Length:* **60 days**
Hybridizer: **unknown**   **1 gallon pot**

photo: Iolanda Marquardt

Aechmea - ornata var. nationalis
Species *-x*   **Collector** *-x*
Size: **30" high**   *Flower Length:* **60 days**
1 gallon pot

photo: Iolanda Marquardt

Aechmea - fendleri
Species -*x*   **Collector -*x***
Size: 32" high   *Flower Length:* 60 days
1 gallon pot

photo: Iolanda Marquardt

Aechmea - rubens
Species -*x*   **Collector -*x***
Size: 48" high   *Flower Length:* 90 days
2 gallon pot

photo: Iolanda Marquardt

Aechmea - 'Yamamoto'
Hybrid -*x*   **Collector -*x***
Size: 18" high   *Flower Length:* 60 days
Hybridizer: Howard Yamamoto   **1 gallon pot**

photo: Iolanda Marquardt

Aechmea - tillandsioides var kienastii
albomarginata
Specie -*x*   **Collector -*x***   **6" pot**
Size: 24 " high   *Flower Length:*   60 days

photo: Iolanda Marquardt

Aechmea - orlandiana 'Ensign'
Specie -x   **Collector -x**
Size: 18" high   *Flower Length:* 60 days
Owner: **E.W. Ensign   6' pot**

photo: Iolanda Marquardt

Aechmea - 'Friederike' (P)
Mutant -x   **Commercial -x**
Size: 24" high   *Flower Length:* 60 days
Bak Collection   1 gallon pot

photo: Iolanda Marquardt

Aechmea - fascini albomarginata
Hybrid -x   **Collector -x**
Size: 30" high   *Flower Length:* 60 days
Hybridizer - K. Williams (Deleon) 1 gallon pot

photo: Iolanda Marquardt

Aechmea - eurycorymbus
Species -x   **Collector -x**
Size: 60" high   *Flower Length:* 90 days
3 gallon pot

21

photo: Iolanda Marquardt

Aechmea - lueddemanniana cv. 'Rodco'
albomarginata (Japan)
Species *-x*   **Collector** *-x*   **1 gallon pot**
Size: **24" high**   ***Flower Length:*** **30 days**

photo: Iolanda Marquardt

Aechmea - 'Eileen' (P)
Hybrid *-x*   ***Commercial*** *-x*
Size: **30" high**   ***Flower Length:*** **60 days**
Hybridizer: **unknown**   **1 gallon pot**

photo: Iolanda Marquardt

Aechmea - ramosa x fulgens
Hybrid-x   ***Commercial*** *-x*
Size: **28" high**   ***Flower Length:*** **45 days**
Hybridizer: **Nat Deleon**   **8" pot**

photo: Iolanda Marquardt

Aechmea - 'Mona'
Hybrid *-x*   ***Collector*** *-x*
Size: **34" high**   ***Flower Length:*** **60 days**
Hybridizer: **F. Buisse**   **2 gallon pot**

22

photo: Iolanda Marquardt

Aechmea - mexicana
Species -x   **Collector -x**   **2 gallon pot**
Size: 36" high   *Flower Length:* **90 days**

photo: Iolanda Marquardt

Aechmea - tessmanii cv. 'Leperosa'
Specie -x   **Collector -x**   **3 gallon pot**
Size: 36" high   *Flower Length:* **90 days**

photo: Iolanda Marquardt

Aechmea - fasciata 'Purple'
Species -x   **Collector -x**
Size: 24" high   *Flower Length:* **30 days**
1 gallon pot

photo: Iolanda Marquardt

Aechmea - araneosa
Species -x   **Collector -x**
Size: 24" high   *Flower Length:* **30 days**
1 gallon pot

photo: Iolanda Marquardt

Aechmea - blanchetiana
Species -x   **Collector -x**
Size: 40" high   *Flower Length:* 3 months
3 gallon pot

photo: Chris Krumrey

Aechmea - chantinni cv. 'Black'
Species -x   **Collector -x**   2 gallon pot
Size: 26" high   *Flower Length:* 1 month

photo: Chris Krumrey

Aechmea - mexicana albomarginata
Species -x   **Collector -x**
Size: 36" high   *Flower Length:* 3 months
3 gallon pot

photo: Ron Parkhuest

Aechmea - nudicaulis var. aureorosea
Species -x   **Collector -x**
Size: 20" high   *Flower Length:* 1 month
1 gallon pot

Billbergia 'De Nada'

photo: Iolanda Marquardi

BILLBERGIA

S. Shiigi 98

Chapter 6

This Bromeliad is named after the Swedish Botanist, Gustave Billberg. Billbergia's are easy to grow, mature fast and reproduce quickly. They have one of the most dynamic, exotic flowers in the Bromeliad family. The only negative is the bloom lasts for approximately one week to two weeks. Besides the short lived flower, what is also attractive about this family is the foliage and shape of the plant. These characteristics make up for any short-term flower they may have. Their shape is tubular and the foliage can be banded, cross bars, spotting and blotching.

This beautiful family came mostly from Brazil and grows on rocks, trees, and on the ground. A real plus for any landscaping design. The average size is approximately 16" or less, though I have seen some in the 2' to 3' range.

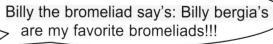

Billy the bromeliad say's: Billy bergia's are my favorite bromeliads!!!

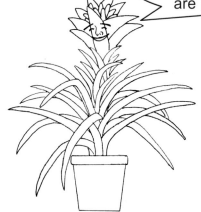

Broneliad seedings growing on coconut husk

photo: Iolanda Marquardi

Billbergia - pyrnamidaus
Species -x   **Collector -x**
Size: 18" high   **Foliage Length:** 6 months
6" pot

Billbergia - 'Pink Champagne'
Hybrid -x   **Collector -x**
Size: 18" high   **Foliage Length:** 6 months
Hybridizer: Joe Carrone   **6" pot**

Billbergia - 'After Glo'
Hybrid -x   **Collector -x**
Size: 18" high   **Foliage Length:** 6 months
Hybridizer: Don Beadle   **6" pot**

Billbergia's - unnamed
Hybrid -x   **Collector -x**
Size: 18" high   **Foliage Length:** 6 months
Hybridizer: Don Beadle   **6"pot**

photo: Iolanda Marquardt

Billbergia - 'De Nada'
Hybrid -x   **Collector -x**
Size: **18" high**   *Foliage Length:* **6 months**
Hybridizer: **Don Beadle   6" pot**

photo: Iolanda Marquardt

Billbergia - '#1238 '
Hybrid -x   **Collector -x**
Size: **18" high**   *Foliage Length:* **6 months**
Hybridizer: **Don Beadle   6" pot**

photo: Iolanda Marquardt

Billbergia - windii
Hybrid -x   **Collector -x**
Size: **18" high**   *Foliage Length:*
Hybridizer: **1800 Europe   6" pot**

photo: Iolanda Marquardt

Billbergia - 'Strawberry'
Hybrid -x   **Collector -x**
Size: **18" high**   *Flower Length:* **6 months**
Hybridizer: **Bruce Thom   6" pot**

photo: Iolanda Marquardt

Billbergia - 'Deliciouso'
Hybrid -x   **Collector -x**
Size: 18" high   **Foliage Length:** 6 months
Hybridizer: Don Beadle   6" pot

photo: Iolanda Marquardt

Billbergia - 'Domingo Martins'
Hybrid -x   **Collector -x**
Size: 18" high   **Foliage Length:** 6 months
Hybridizer: Bob Whitman (Beadle)   6" pot

photo: Christopher Krumrey

Billbergia - 'Poquito Mas '
Hybrid -x   **Collector -x**
Size: 18" high   **Foliage Length:** 6 months
Hybridizer: Don Beadle   6" pot

photo: Christopher Krumrey

Billbergia - 'Mamie B'
Hybrid -x   **Collector -x**
Size: 18" high   **Foliage Length:** 6 months
Hybridizer: Don Beadle   6" pot

photo: Christopher Krumrey

Billbergia - *'Hallelujah'*
Hybrid -x   **Collector -x**
Size: 18" high   **Foliage Length:** 6 months
Hybridizer: Don Beadle   6" pot

photo: Christopher Krumrey

Billbergia - *'Estrella'*
Hybrid -x   **Collector -x**
Size: 18" high   **Foliage Length:** 6 months
Hybridizer: Don Beadle   6" pot

photo: Christopher Krumrey

Billbergia - *'Dilicoso'*
Hybrid -x   **Collector -x**
Size: 18" high   **Foliage Length:** 6 months
Hybridizer: Don Beadle   6" pot

photo: Christopher Krumrey

Billbergia - *'Pink Champagne'*
Hybrid -x   **Collector -x**
Size: 18" high   **Foliage Length:** 6 months
Hybridizer: Carrona   6" pot

photo: Christopher Krumrey

Billbergia - **'Primavera'**
Hybrid -x   *Collector -x*
Size: **18" high**   *Foliage Length:* **6 months**
Hybridizer: **Don Beadle**   **6" pot**

photo: Christopher Krumrey

Billbergia - **'Violetta'**
Hybrid -x   *Collector -x*
Size: **18" high**   *Foliage Length:* **6 months**
Hybridizer: **Don Beadle**   **6" pot**

photo: Christopher Krumrey

Billbergia -   **'Sangre'**
Hybrid -x   *Collector -x*
Size: **18" high**   *Foliage Length:* **6 months**
Hybridizer: **Don Beadle**   **6" pot**

photo: Christopher Krumrey

Billbergia - **'Catherine Wilson'**
Hybrid   *Collector*
Size: **18" high**   *Foliage Length:* **6 months**
Hybridizer: **Wilson**   **6" pot**

31

photo: Christopher Krumrey

Billbergia - *'Luna Blanca'*
Hybrid *-x*   **Collector** *-x*
Size: 18" high   **Foliage Length:** 6 months
Hybridizer: Don Beadle   6" pot

photo: Christopher Krumrey

Billbergia - *'Baton Rouge'*
Hybrid *-x*   **Collector** *-x*
Size: 18" high   **Foliage Length:** 6 months
Hybridizer: Don Beadle   6" pot

photo: Iolanda Marquardi

Billbergia - *'Domineos Martins'*
Hybrid *-x*   **Collector** *-x*
Size: 16" high   **Foliage Length:** 6 months
Hybridizer: B. Whitman (Beadle)   6" pot

photo: Christopher Krumrey

Billbergia - *'Afterglow'*
Hybrid *-x*   **Collector** *-x*
Size: 20" high   **Foliage Length:** 6 months
Hybridizer: Don Beadle   6" pot

Billbergia - 'Hallelujah'

33

Cryptanthus - 'Black Beauty'

photo: Iolanda Marquardt

CRYPTANTHUS

Chapter 7

Cryptanthus means, "hidden flowers" and was named by a German, Mr. Klotzch, in the 1830's, and was grown in England in the 1820's. Again, this Bromeliad can be found in Brazil with approximately 100 species. It is a terrestrial, meaning it gets nutrients from its roots and grows in the ground.

We have found that Cryptanthus does not like our regular potting mix, but prefers spagnum moss and lots of water. Because of their shape and markings, they have been nicknamed "earth stars" and "lizard plants".

Their size is small to medium, with a span of approximately 12" or less. They grow low to the ground with heights lower than 6". Colors are browns, black, gray, green, purples, pinks, reds, silver, varigated and albomarginata. Markings include bands, zigzags, bars, stripes and mottling. The offshoots are produced by basal/offsets, between the leaves and underground stolons. The flowers (usually small and white) are not the objects of the plant. It is their unusual shape and foliage that is the attraction of this family. It enhances any landscape or interiorscape design. This is the only family that has it's own society, "the Cryptanthus Society" and we recommend that you join this society, which has a quarterly publication. Light requirements are from bright-defused light to low light.

Billy the bromeliad says's: Why don't they bury bromeliads in the ground after they die? Because they put them in a cryptanthus!

Cryptanthus
'Elaine' Albomarginata

photo: CHRISTOPHER KRUMREY

photo: Iolanda Marquardt

Cryptanthus - zonatus 'Silver'
Specie -x   **Collector -x**
Size: 10" wide   **Foliage Length:** 6 months +
Owner: J. Arlety   4" pot

photo: Iolanda Marquardt

Cryptanthus - 'Arlety'
Hybrid -x   **Commercial -x**
Size: 10" wide   **Foliage Length:** 6 months +
Hybridizer: J. Arlety   4" pot

photo: Iolanda Marquardt

Cryptanthus - fosterianas
Specie -x   **Collector -x**   4" pot
Size: 10" wide   **Foliage Length:** 6 months +

photo: Iolanda Marquardt

Cryptanthus - Unnamed
Hybrid -x   **Collector -x**
Size: 10" wide   **Foliage Length:** 6 months +
Owner: Ron Parkhurst   4" pot

photo: Iolanda Marquardt

Cryptanthus - acaulis
Specie -x   **Collector -x**
Size: **10" wide**   *Foliage Length:* **6 months +**
Owner: **Ron Parkhurst   4" pot**

photo: Iolanda Marquardt

Cryptanthus - Unnamed
Hybrid -x   **Collector -x**
Size: **10" wide**   *Flower Length:* **6 months +**
Owner: **Ron Parkhurst   4" pot**

photo: Iolanda Marquardt

Cryptanthus - 'Christmas Cheer'
Hybrid -x   **Collector -x**
Size: **10" wide**   *Flower Length:* **6 months +**
Hybridizer: **Garretson   4" pot**

photo: Iolanda Marquardt

Cryptanthus - Unnamed
Hybrid -x   **Collector -x**
Size: **10" wide**   *Flower Length:* **6 months +**
Owner: **Ron Parkhurst   4" pot**

photo: Iolanda Marquardt

Cryptanthus - Unknown
Hybrid -x　　**Collector -x**
Size: 10" wide　**Foliage Length:** 6 months +
Hybridizer: Unknown　　4" pot

photo: Iolanda Marquardt

Cryptanthus - 'Iron Age'
Hybrid -x　　**Collector -x**
Size: 10" wide　**Foliage Length:** 6 months +
Hybridizer: Dorr　　4" pot

photo: Iolanda Marquardt

Cryptanthus - 'Hawaiian Sunrise'
Hybrid -x　　**Collector -x**
Size: 10" wide　**Foliage Length:** 6 months +
Hybridizer: Richard Lum　4" pot

photo: Ron Parkhurst

Cryptanthus - 'Arlety'
Hybrid -x　　**Collector -x**
Size: 10" wide　**Flowere Length:** 6 months +
Owner: J. Arlety　　4" pot

photo: Iolanda Marquardt

Cryptanthus - acaulis abomarginata
Specie -x   ***Collector -x***
***Size:* 10" wide   *Foliage Length:* 6 months +**
***Owner:* Unknown   4" pot**

photo: Iolanda Marquardt

Cryptanthus - 'Black Beauty'
Hybrid -x   ***Collector -x***
***Size:* 10" wide   *Foliage Length:* 6 months +**
***Hybridizer:* Baensch   4" pot**

photo: Iolanda Marquardt

Cryptanthus - Unnamed
Hybrid -x   ***Collector -x***
***Size:* 10" wide   *Flowere Length:* 6 months +**
***Owner:* Ron Parkhurst   4" pot**

photo: Christopher Kromrey

Cryptanthus - 'Durrell'
Hybrid -x   ***Collector -x***
***Size:* 10" wide   *Flowere Length:* 6 months +**
***Hybridizer:* Irvin   4" pot**

photo: Christopher Kromrey

Cryptanthus - 'Corinne'
Hybrid -x   **Collector -x**
Size: 8" wide   *Foliage Length:* 6 months +
Hybridizer: Dupuy   4" pot

photo: Christopher Kromrey

Cryptanthus - 'Earth Angel'
Hybrid -x   **Collector -x**
Size: 10" wide   *Foliage Length:* 6 months +
Hybridizer: Richtmyer   4" pot

photo: Christopher Kromrey

Cryptanthus - 'Beau Brummel'
Hybrid -x   **Collector -x**
Size: 10" wide   *Foliage Length:* 6 months +
Hybridizer: Antie   4" pot

photo: Christopher Kromrey

Cryptanthus - bahianus var virdis
Specie -x   **Collector -x**   4" pot
Size: 10" wide   *Foliage Length:* 6 months +

photo: Christopher Kromrey

Cryptanthus - beuckeri x bahianus
Hybrid -x   **Collector -x**
Size: 8" wide   *Foliage Length:* 6 months +
Hybridizer: unknown   4" pot

photo: Christopher Kromrey

Cryptanthus - 'Dark Beauty'
Hybrid -x   **Collector -x**
Size: 10" wide   *Foliage Length:* 6 months +
Hybridizer: Goode   4" pot

photo: Christopher Kromrey

Cryptanthus - bivittatus - major
Specie -x   **Collector -x**
Size: 10" wide   *Foliage Length:* 6 months +
          4" pot

photo: Christopher Kromrey

Cryptanthus- 'Ulla Colin'
Hybrid -x   **Collector -x**
Size: 10" wide   *Foliage Length:* 6 months +
Hybridizer: Colin   4" pot

photo: Christopher Kromrey

Cryptanthus - 'Fire Blush'
Hybrid -x   **Collector -x**
Size: **8" wide**   *Foliage Length:* **6 months +**
Hybridizer: **Dorr**   **4" pot**

photo: Christopher Kromrey

Cryptanthus - bahianus 'Rubia'
Specie -x   **Collector -x**
Size: **10" wide**   *Foliage Length:* **6 months +**
4" pot

photo: Christopher Kromrey

Cryptanthus - 'Pixie'
Hybrid -x   **Collector -x**
Size: **10" wide**   *Foliage Length:* **6 months +**
Hybridizer: **Irvin**   **4" pot**

photo: Christopher Kromrey

Cryptanthus - 'Jimmy Antle'
Hybrid -x   **Collector -x**
Size: **10" wide**   *Foliage Length:* **6 months +**
Hybridizer: **Antle**   **4" pot**

photo: Christopher Kromrey

Cryptanthus - zonantis 'Silver'
Hybrid -x **Collector -x**
Size: **10" wide** *Foliage Length:* **6 months +**
Hybridizer: **Colin** **4" pot**

photo: Christopher Kromrey

Cryptanthus - 'Strawberry Flambe'
Hybrid -x **Collector -x**
Size: **10" wide** *Foliage Length:* **6 months +**
Hybridizer: **Schrenker** **4" pot**

photo: Christopher Kromrey

Cryptanthus - 'Rose Glow'
Hybrid -x **Collector -x**
Size: **10" wide** *Foliage Length:* **6 months +**
Hybridizer: **Ruthedge** **4" pot**

photo: Christopher Kromrey

Cryptanthus - 'Silver Sheen' x 'Timothy Plow'
Hybrid -x **Collector -x**
Size: **10" wide** *Foliage Length:* **6 months +**
Hybridizer: **Colin** **4" pot**

Cryptanthus - 'Irish Mist'
Hybrid -x   *Collector -x*
Size: **8" wide**
Foliage Length: **6 months +**
Hybridizer: **Irvin**
4" pot

photo: Christopher Kromrey

Cryptanthus -bivittatus
Specie -x   **Collector -x**
Size: **8" wide**
Foliage Length: **6 months +**
4" pot

photo: Christopher Kromrey

Guzmania -'Super Alii' (PP)

photo: Iolanda Marquardi

45

GUZMANIA

Chapter 8

This bromeliad was named after Anastasio Guzman an eighteenth century Spanish naturalist. There are approximately 125 species and hundreds of hybrids in this family. Guzmania's are probably the number one interior plant and one of my favorite plants in the bromeliad world.

Guzmania's, Tillandsia's and Vriesea's are similar in many ways. One of the main differences is that Tillandsia's and Vriesea's have disticaous flowers (flowers arranged in two rows). On the other hand, Guzmania's flower spikes are always polystichous (spikes radiate from all sides of the axis).

This family is found mainly in Columbia and Ecuador. They grow anywhere from sea level to 10,000 ft., but thrive in warm, humid temperatures. Indirect sunlight and good air movement, make a perfect environment.

The infloresence is the main attraction here, though some Guzmania's have very attractive leaves, especially Guzmania's Sanguinea, which has a bright red, orange, and yellow leaf only at flowering time. Other foliage colors can include some colors, but generally are mostly green. They are also thornless.

Again, the size range varies from small (6" to 30" height) to over three feet in width. Most of the Guzmania's are in the medium range (16" to 18" height). Flowers will last 30 to 90 days on the average, and are excellent indoor plants used in various designs.

Billy the bromeliad says; rose's are red, violets are blue, bromeliads have far more colors; than most people knew!!!

photo: David Shiigi

Guzmania - Monostachia variegata
Specie -x   *Commercial -x*   **6" pot**
Size: **24" high**   *Flower Length:* **90 days**

photo: Iolanda Marquardt

Guzmania - Bigeneric guz ./vr.
Hybrid -x   *Collector -x*
Size: **12" high**   *Flower Length:* **90 days**
Hybridizer: **unknown**   **6" pot**

photo: Iolanda Marquardt

Guzmania - 'Super Alii' (PP)
Hybrid -x   *Commercial -x*
Size: **24" high**   *Flower Length:* **90 days**
Hybridizer: **David Shiigi**   **6" pot**

photo: Iolanda Marquardt

Guzmania - 'Alii' (PP)
Hybrid -x   *Commercial -x*
Size: **24" high**   *Flower Length:* **90 days**
Hybridizer: **David Shiigi**   **6" pot**

47

photo: Iolanda Marquardit

Guzmania - 'Puna Gold' variegata
Mutant -x   Collector -x
Size: 24" high   *Flower Length:* 90 days
Hybridizer: David Shiigi   6" pot

photo: Iolanda Marquardt

Guzmania - 'Super Puna Gold' (PP)
Hybrid -x   Commercial -x
Size: 24" high   *Flower Length:* 90 days
Hybridizer: David Shiigi   6" pot

photo: Iolanda Marquardt

Guzmania - 'Puna Gold '(P)
Hybrid -x   Commercial -x
Size: 24" high   *Flower Length:* 90 days
Hybridizer: David Shiigi   6" pot

photo:Ron Parkhurst

Guzmania - 'Red Maui Sunset'
Mutant -x   Collector -x
Size: 24" high   *Flower Length:* 90 days
Owner: Ron Parkhurst   6" pot

48

Guzmania - 'Yellow Denise'
Mutant -x   **Collector -x**
Size: **18" high**   *Flower Length:* **90 days**
Owner: **Ron Parkhurst   6" pot**

Guzmania - 'Zahnii'
Specie -x   **Collector -x   6" pot**
Size: **24" high**   *Flower Length:* **90 days**

Guzmania - 'Kahili'
Hybrid -x   **Collector -x**
Size: **30" high**   *Flower Length:* **90 days**
Hybridizer: **Tsuro Murakami   6" pot**

Guzmania - 'Super Kapoho Flame' (PP)
Hybrid -x   **Commercial -x**
Size: **24" high**   *Flower Length:* **90 days**
Hybridizer: **David Shiigi   6" pot**

49

photo: Iolanda Marquardt

Guzmania - 'Kapoho Flame' (PP)
Hybrid -x   *Commercial -x*
Size: **24" high**   *Flower Length:* **90 days**
Hybridizer: **David Shiigi**   **6" pot**

photo: Ron Parkhurst

Guzmania - New Cultivar of Quinn
Mutant -x   *Collector -x*
Size: **24" high**   *Flower Length:* **90 days**
Owner: **Ron Parkhurst**   **6" pot**

photo: Ron Parkhurst

Guzmania - New Cultivar of 'Denise'
Mutant -x   *Collector -x*
Size: **24" high**   *Flower Length:* **90 days**
Owner: **Ron Parkhurst**   **6" pot**

photo: Iolanda Marquardt

Guzmania - 'Moonlight'
Mutant -x   *Collector -x*
Size: **24" high**   *Flower Length:* **90 days**
Owner: **Unknown 6" pot**

photo: Iolanda Marquardt

Guzmania - 'White Grapeade'
Mutant *-x*   **Collector** *-x*
Size: 24" high   **Flower Length:** 90 days
Owner: Ron Parkhurst   6" pot

photo: Iolanda Marquardt

Guzmania - 'Purple'
Hybrid *-x*   **Collector** *-x*
Size: 24" high   **Flower Length:** 90 days
Owner: Ron Parkhurst   6" pot

photo: Iolanda Marquardt

Guzmania - 'Luna'
Hybrid *-x*   **Commercial** *-x*
Size: 24" high   **Flower Length:** 90 days
Hybridizer: BAK   6" pot

photo: Iolanda Marquardt

Guzmania - 'Grand Prix' "Purple"
Mutant *-x*   **Collector** *-x*
Size: 24" high   **Flower Length:** 90 days
Owner: Ron Parkhurst   6" pot

photo: Iolanda Marquardt

Guzmania - 'Purple'
Hybrid -x   *Collector -x*
Size: **24" high**   *Flower Length:* **90 days**
Owner: **Ron Parkhurst**   **6" pot**

photo: Iolanda Marquardt

Guzmania - 'Grapeade'
Mutant -x   *Collector -x*
Size: **24" high**   *Flower Length:* **90 days**
Owner: **Ron Parkhurst**   **6" pot**

photo: Iolanda Marquardt

Guzmania - 'Maui Sunset' (PP)
Mutant -x   *Commercial -x*
Size: **24" high**   *Flower Length:* **90 days**
Owner: **Ron Parkhurst**   **6" pot**

photo: Iolanda Marquardt

Guzmania - 'Maui Sunrise'
Mutant -x   *Collector -x*
Size: **24" high**   *Flower Length:* **90 days**
Owner: **Ron Parkhurst**   **6" pot**

Guzmania -'Orangeade'
Hybrid -x   *Commercial -x*
Size: 24" high   *Flower Length:* 90 days
Hybridizer: Demeyer   6" pot

Guzmania - 'Orange' variegata
Mutant -x   *Collector -x*
Size: 24" high   *Flower Length:* 90 days
Owner: Ron Parkhurst   6" pot

Guzmania - 'Variegated Yellow'
Mutant -x   *Collector -x*
Size: 24" high   *Flower Length:* 90 days
Owner: Ron Parkhurst   6" pot

Guzmania - 'Ostara'
Hybrid -x   *Commercial -x*
Size: 24" high   *Flower Length:* 90 days
Owner: BAK   6" pot

53

photo: Iolanda Marquardt

Guzmania -unnamed
Mutant -x   *Collector -x*
Size: 24" high   *Flower Length:* 90 days
Owner: Ron Parkhurst   6" pot

photo: Iolanda Marquardt

Guzmania - 'Claret'
Hybrid -x   *Commercial -x*
Size: 20" high   *Flower Length:* 90 days
Hybridizer: BAK   6" pot

photo: Iolanda Marquardt

Guzmania - 'Denise'
Hybrid -x   *Commercial -x*
Size: 24" high   *Flower Length:* 90 days
Hybridizer: BAK   6" pot

photo: Iolanda Marquardt

Guzmania - 'Grand Prix'
Hybrid -x   *Commercial -x*
Size: 24" high   *Flower Length:* 90 days
Hybridizer: BAK   6" pot

photo: Iolanda Marquardt

Guzmania - 'Starfire'
Hybrid -x   *Commercial -x*
Size: 24" high   *Flower Length:* 90 days
Hybridizer: Deleon   6" pot

photo: Iolanda Marquardt

Guzmania - 'Watermelon'
Hybrid -x   *Commercial -x*
Size: 24" high   *Flower Length:* 90 days
Hybridizer: Unknown   6" pot

photo: Iolanda Marquardt

Guzmania - Assortment
Hybrid-x   *Commercial -x*
Size: 24" high   *Flower Length:* 90 days
Owner: Ron Parkhurst   6" pot

photo: Iolanda Marquardt

Guzmania - 'Tutti-fruitti'
Hybrid -x   *Commercial -x*
Size: 24" high   *Flower Length:* 90 days
Hybridizer: Demeyer - DeRouck   6" pot

photo: Iolanda Marquardt

Guzmania - 'Morado' (P)
Hybrid -x   *Commercial -x*
Size: 30" high   *Flower Length:* 90 days
Hybridizer: BAK   6" pot

photo: Iolanda Marquardt

Guzmania - lingulata "Purple"
Hybrid -x   *Collector -x*
Size: 12" high   *Flower Length:* 90 days
Owner: Ron Parkhurst   6" pot

photo: Iolanda Marquardt

Guzmania - 'Ultra' (P)
Hybrid -x   *Commercial -x*
Size: 8" high   *Flower Length:* 90 days
Hybridizer: BAK   4" pot

photo: Iolanda Marquardt

Guzmania - 'Carine'
Hybrid -x   *Commercial -x*
Size: 8" high   *Flower Length:* 90 days
Hybridizer: Demeyer - DeRouck   6" pot

photo: Iolanda Marquardt

Guzmania - wittmackii cv 'Blush'
Hybrid -x   *Collector -x*
Size: 36" high   *Flower Length:* 90 days
Owner: Ron Parkhurst   7" pot

photo: Iolanda Marquardt

Guzmania - wittmackii cv 'Mini Purple'
Hybrid -x   *Collector -x*
Size: 14" high   *Flower Length:* 90 days
Owner: Ron Parkhurst   6" pot

photo: Iolanda Marquardt

Guzmania - wittmackii 'Mini Rose'
Hybrid -x   *Collector -x*
Size: 14" high   *Flower Length:* 90 days
Owner: Ron Parkhurst   6" pot

photo: Iolanda Marquardt

Guzmania - wittmackii 'Purple'
Hybrid -x   *Collector -x*
Size: 30" high   *Flower Length:* 90 days
Owner: Ron Parkhurst   7" pot

photo: Iolanda Marquardt

Guzmania - wittmackii 'Yellow'
Hybrid -x   *Collector -x*
Size: 30" high   *Flower Length:* 90 days
Owner: Ron Parkhurst   7" pot

photo: Iolanda Marquardt

Guzmania - wittmackii 'Red'
Hybrid -x   *Collector -x*
Size: 36" high   *Flower Length:* 90 days
Owner: Ron Parkhurst   7" pot

photo: Iolanda Marquardt

Guzmania - wittmackii 'Pink'
Hybrid -x   *Collector -x*
Size: 36" high   *Flower Length:* 90 days
Owner: Ron Parkhurst   7" pot

photo: Ron Parkhurst

Guzmania - wittmackii 'Sherbert'
Hybrid -x   *Collector -x*
Size: 30" high   *Flower Length:* 90 days
Owner: Ron Parkhurst   7" pot

photo: Ron Parkhurst

Guzmania - 'Crimson'
Hybrid -x   *Collector -x*
Size: 30" high   *Flower Length:* 90 days
Owner: Ron Parkhurst   6" pot

photo: Ron Parkhurst

Guzmania - squarrosa
Specie -x   *Collector -x*   6" pot
Size: 24" high   *Flower Length:* 90 days

photo: Ron Parkhurst

Guzmania - 'Magenta'
Hybrid -x   *Collector -x*
Size: 30" high   *Flower Length:* 90 days
Owner: Ron Parkhurst   6" pot

photo: Ron Parkhurst

Guzmania - 'White Lightning'
Hybrid -x   *Collector -x*
Size: 36" high   *Flower Length:* 90 days
Owner: Ron Parkhurst   7" pot

photo: Ron Parkhurst

Guzmania - 'Torch' (P)
Hybrid -x   *Commercial -x*
Size: 24" high   *Flower Length:* 90 days
Hybridizer: BAK   6" pot

photo: Ron Parkhurst

Guzmania - 'Carine' x lingulata 'Cross'
Hybrid -x   *Collector -x*
Size: 20" high   *Flower Length:* 90 days
Hybridizer: David Shiigi   6" pot

photo: Ron Parkhurst

Guzmania - wittmackii 'Sunset'
Hybrid -x   *Collector -x*
Size: 30" high   *Flower Length:* 90 days
Owner: Ron Parkhurst   7" pot

photo: Ron Parkhurst

Guzmania - lingulata variegata
Mutant -x   *Collector -x*
Size: 14" high   *Flower Length:* 60 days
Owner: Unknown   6" pot

Guzmania - wittmackii 'Mini Sunset'
Hybrid *-x*   **Collector** *-x*
Size: 14" high   **Flower Length:** 90 days
Owner: Ron Parkhurst   6" pot

Guzmania - 'Purple Squarrosa'
Hybrid *-x*   **Collector** *-x*
Size: 20" high   **Flower Length:** 90 days
Owner: Ron Parkhurst   6" pot

Guzmania - 'Squarrosa Sunrise'
Mutant *-x*   **Collector** *-x*
Size: 24" high   **Flower Length:** 90 days
Owner: Ron Parkhurst   6" pot

Guzmania - 'Purple'
Hybrid *-x*   **Collector** *-x*
Size: 26" high   **Flower Length:** 90 days
Owner: Ron Parkhurst   6" pot

photo: Ron Parkhurst

Guzmania - 'Super Purple'
Hybrid -x   *Collector -x*
Size: **26" high**   *Flower Length:* **90 days**
Hybridizer: **Unknown**   **7" pot**

photo: Ron Parkhurst

Guzmania - Unnamed
Hybrid -x   *Collector -x*
Size: **24" high**   *Flower Length:* **90 days**
Hybridizer: **Ron Parkhurst**   **6" pot**

photo: Chris Krumrey

Guzmania - 'Graaf Van Horn'
Hybrid -x   *Collector -x*
Size: **30" high**   *Flower Length:* **120days**
Owner: **Deroose**   **6" pot**

photo: Chris Krumrey

Guzmania - 'Gisela Don Pepe'
Mutant -x   *Collector -x*
Size: **130" high**   *Flower Length:* **90 days**
Owner: **Deroose**   **6" pot**

photo: Ron Parkhurst

Guzmania - 'Squarrosa Sunrise'

photo: Ron Parkhurst

Guzmania - 'Denise'

63

Neoregelia - 'Ninja'

photo: Iolanda Marquardt

NEOREGELIA

Chapter 9

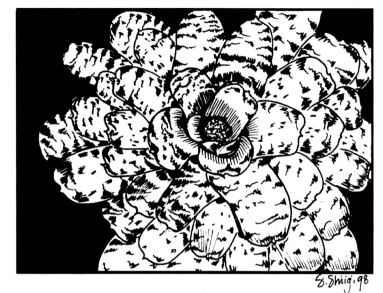

S.Shiigi.98

The "Neos" as they are nicknamed have approximately 100 species. They are found in Brazil, Columbia and Peru. They were named in the 19th century by Russian botanist, Edward Von Regal. They grow naturally near the lower levels of the rain forest on fallen trees or lower branches. Some grow saxicolously (on rocks) in full sun.

This is another favorite family of mine. This bromeliad is mainly for foliage, color, shape and conformation of the leaves. It is also a favorite with hybridizers. The wide selection of color is one of the main reasons, along with the shape. Neo's off/set any bromeliad design, whether inside or outside, and are very attractive by themselves. The inflorescence is a rosette shape and stays in the center of the plant's cup. Tiny flowers rise out of the rosette and range in color from blue, white and purple.

Again size varies from miniatures, 4 inches in diameter to as large as 4 feet in diameter. Leaves may be green, silver scales, banded, variegated, marbled, spotted, albomarginata, reds, purples, pinks and blues. Leaf tips can be pointed, rounded, symmetrical and spiral in formation.

One of the best ways to get good results from growing neo's is to give them a good start with fertilizer and mix. As they grow into maturity, we cease to fertilize and move them into more light, keeping the plant more compact and intensifying the color in the leaves.

Billy the bromeliad says; if Neo married Regelia and they had a baby girl, what would they name her? Elizabeth! (Bet you thought I'd say Neoregelia!)

photo: Iolanda Marquardt

Neoregelia - 'Oeser 100'
Hybrid -x   **Collector -x**
Size: 14" wide   ***Foliage Length:* 6 months**
Hybridizer: Dr. Oeser   6" pot

photo: Iolanda Marquardt

Neoregelia - 'Kahala Dawn'
Hybrid -x   **Collector -x**
Size: 14" wide   ***Foliage Length:* 6 months**
Owner: Bob Okazaki   6" pot

photo: Iolanda Marquardt

Neoregelia - Unnamed
Hybrid -x   **Collector -x**
Size: 14" wide   ***Foliage Length:* 6 months**
Hybridizer: Hatsumi Maertz   6" pot

photo: Iolanda Marquardt

Neoregelia - 'Debbie'
Hybrid -x   **Collector -x**
Size: 14" wide   ***Foliage Length:* 6 months**
Hybridizer: Grant Groves   6" pot

Neoregelia - 'Oeser 100' variation
Hybrid *-x*   **Collector** *-x*
Size: 14" wide   **Foliage Length:** 6 months
Owner: Dr. Oeser   6" pot

Neoregelia - Johannis cv. 'Pink Tips'
Specie *-x*   **Collector** *-x*   6" pot
Size: 14" wide   **Foliage Length:** 6 months

Neoregelia - concentrica var. albomarginata
Specie *-x*   **Collector** *-x*   6" pot
Size: 14" wide   **Foliage Length:** 6 months

Neoregelia - 'Charm'
Hybrid *-x*   **Collector** *-x*
Size: 14" wide   **Foliage Length:** 6 months
Hybridizer: Grace Goode   6" pot

photo: Iolanda Marquardt

Neoregelia - unnamed
Hybrid -x   ***Collector -x***
***Size:* 14" wide**   ***Foliage Length:* 6 months**
***Hybrider:* David Shiigi**   6" pot

photo: Iolanda Marquardt

Neoregelia - 'Manoa Beauty '
Hybrid -x   ***Collector -x***
***Size:* 14" wide**   ***Foliage Length:* 6 months**
***Hybridizer:* Mike Yamamoto**   6" pot

photo: Iolanda Marquardt

Neoregelia - Group of 'Debbie'
Hybrid -x   ***Collector -x***
***Size:* 14" wide**   ***Foliage Length:* 6 months**
***Hybridizer:* Grant Groves**   6" pot

photo: Iolanda Marquardt

Neoregelia - Group of 'Ninja'
Hybrid -x   ***Collector -x***
***Size:* 14" wide**   ***Foliage Length:* 6 months**
***Hybridizer:* David Shiigi**   6" pot

photo: Iolanda Marquardt

Neoregelia - 'Van Dorme' albomarginata
Hybrid -x   **Collector -x**
Size: 14" wide   **Foliage Length: 6 months**
Hybridizer: **F. Gruber**   6" pot

photo: Iolanda Marquardt

Neoregelia - 'Scarlet Charlotte
Hybrid -x   **Collector -x**
Size: 14" wide   **Foliage Length: 6 months**
Hybridizer: **Grant Groves**   6" pot

photo: Iolanda Marquardt

Neoregelia - 'Oeser 100'
Hybrid -x   **Collector -x**
Size: 14" wide   **Foliage Length: 6 months**
Hybridizer: **Dr. Oeser**   6" pot

photo: Iolanda Marquardt

Neoregelia - fireball
Species -x   *Collector -x 4" pot*
Size: 6" wide   **Foliage Length: 6 months**

photo: Iolanda Marquardt

Neoregelia - 'Fireball' albomarginata
Mutant -x   **Collector -x**
Size: **6" wide**   *Foliage Length:* **6 months**
Owner: **Chester Skotak   4" pot**

photo: Iolanda Marquardt

Neoregelia - 'Grace x Passion'
Hybrid -x   **Collector -x**
Size: **18" wide**   *Foliage Length:* **6 months**
Hybridizer: **Grant Groves   8" pot**

photo: Iolanda Marquardt

Neoregelia - melonodonta x 'Ninja'
Hybrid -x   **Collector -x**
Size: **14" wide**   *Foliage Length:* **6 months**
Hybridizer: **David Shiigi   6" pot**

photo: Iolanda Marquardt

Neoregelia - Unnamed
Hybrid -x   **Collector -x**
Size: **14" wide**   *Foliage Length:* **6 months**
Hybridizer: **David Shiigi   6" pot**

photo: Iolanda Marquardt

Neoregelia - Unnamed
Hybrid -x   **Collector -x**
Size: 14" wide   **Foliage Length: 6 months**
Hybridizer: **David Shiigi**   6" pot

photo: Iolanda Marquardt

Neoregelia - 'Metalica'
Hybrid -x   **Collector -x**
Size: 14" wide   **Foliage Length: 6 months**
Hybridizer: **David Shiigi**   6" pot

photo: Iolanda Marquardt

Neoregelia - Unnamed
Hybrid -x   **Collector -x**
Size: 14" wide   **Foliage Length: 6 months**
Hybridizer: **David Shiigi**   6" pot

photo: Iolanda Marquardt

Neoregelia - Unnamed
Hybrid -x   **Collector -x**
Size: 14" wide   **Foliage Length: 6 months**
Hybridizer: **David Shiigi**   6" pot

photo: Iolanda Marquardt

Neoregelia - 'Princess Kaiulani'
Hybrid -x   ***Collector -x***
Size: **14" wide**   ***Foliage Length:*** **6 months**
Hybridizer: **David Shiigi**   6" pot

photo: Iolanda Marquardt

Neoregelia - 'Prince Kuhio'
Hybrid -x   ***Collector -x***
Size: **14" wide**   ***Foliage Length:*** **6 months**
Hybridizer: **David Shiigi**   6" pot

photo: Iolanda Marquardt

Neoregelia - 'Hawaiian Rain Forest'
Hybrid -x   ***Collector -x***
Size: **14" wide**   ***Foliage Length:*** **6 months**
Hybridizer: **David Shiigi**   6" pot

photo: Iolanda Marquardt

Neoregelia - 'Ninja' cultivar
Hybrid -x   ***Collector -x***
Size: **14" wide**   ***Foliage Length:*** **6 months**
Hybridizer: **David Shiigi**   6" pot

photo: Iolanda Marquardt

Neoregelia - 'Kapoho'
Hybrid *-x*   **Collector** *-x*
Size: **14" wide**   *Foliage Length:* **6 months**
Hybridizer: **David Shiigi**   6" pot

photo: Iolanda Marquardt

Neoregelia - 'Bill Kirker'
Hybrid *-x*   **Collector** *-x*
Size: **14" wide**   *Foliage Length:* **6 months**
Hybridizer: **David Shiigi**   6" pot

photo: Iolanda Marquardt

Neoregelia - 'Toshiya'
Hybrid *-x*   **Collector** *-x*
Size: **14" wide**   *Foliage Length:* **6 months**
Hybridizer: **David Shiigi**   6" pot

photo: Iolanda Marquardt

Neoregelia - 'Ninja' cultivar
Hybrid *-x*   **Collector** *-x*
Size: **14" wide**   *Foliage Length:* **6 months**
Hybridizer: **David Shiigi**   6" pot

photo: Iolanda Marquardt

Neoregelia - 'Ninja' variation
Hybrid *-x*   **Collector** *-x*
Size: 10" wide   **Foliage Length:** 6 months
Hybridizer: David Shiigi   6" pot

photo: Iolanda Marquardt

Neoregelia - 'Ninja' variation
Hybrid *-x*   **Collector** *-x*
Size: 10" wide   **Foliage Length:** 6 months
Hybridizer: David Shiigi   6" pot

photo: Iolanda Marquardt

Neoregelia - 'Hawaiian Princess'
Hybrid *-x*   **Collector** *-x*
Size: 14" wide   **Foliage Length:** 6 months
Hybridizer: David Shiigi   6" pot

photo: Iolanda Marquardt

Neoregelia - 'Painter Delight'
Hybrid *-x*   **Collector** *-x*
Size: 14" wide   **Foliage Length:** 6 months
Hybridizer: Bill Kirker   6" pot

photo: Iolanda Marquardt

Neoregelia - 'Ron Parkhurst' (just kidding David!)
Hybrid -x   **Collector -x**
Size: 14" wide   **Foliage Length:** 6 months
Hybridizer: David Shiigi   6" pot

photo: Iolanda Marquardt

Neoregelia - Unnamed
Hybrid -x   **Collector -x**
Size: 14" wide   **Foliage Length:** 6 months
Hybridizer: David Shiigi   6" pot

photo: Iolanda Marquardt

Neoregelia - Group of Concentrica + 'Ninja' Hybrids
Hybrid -x   **Collector-x**
Size: 14" wide   **Foliage Length:** 6 months
Hybridizer: David Shiigi   6" pot

photo: Iolanda Marquardt

Neoregelia - 'Pink Sensation'
Hybrid -x   **Collector-x**
Size: 14" wide   **Foliage Length:** 6 months
Hybridizer: Grant Groves   6" pot

photo: Iolanda Marquardt

Neoregelia - 'Patrice Parkhurst' (just kidding David!)
Hybrid -x   *Collector-x*
Size: **14" wide**   *Foliage Length:* **6 months**
Hybridizer: **David Shiigi**   **6" pot**

photo: Iolanda Marquardt

Neoregelia - 'Takamura Grande'
Hybrid -x   *Collector-x*
Size: **14" wide**   *Foliage Length:* **6 months**
Hybridizer: **Richter (R. Davis)**   **6" pot**

photo: Iolanda Marquardt

Neoregelia - 'Elizabeth Parkhurst' (just kidding David!)
Hybrid -x   *Collector-x*
Size: **14" wide**   *Foliage Length:* **6 months**
Hybridizer: **David Shiigi**   **6" pot**

photo: Iolanda Marquardt

Neoregelia - Unnamed
Hybrid -x   *Collector-x*
Size: **14" wide**   *Foliage Length:* **6 months**
Hybridizer: **David Shiigi**   **6" pot**

photo: Iolanda Marquardt

Neoregelia - Unnamed
Hybrid -x   **Collector-x**
Size: **14" wide**   *Foliage Length:* **6 months**
Hybridizer: **David Shiigi`**   6" pot

photo: Iolanda Marquardt

Neoregelia - 'Pele'
Hybrid -x   **Collector-x**
Size: **14" wide**   *Foliage Length:* **6 months**
Hybridizer: **David Shiigi**   6" pot

photo: Iolanda Marquardt

Neoregelia - Unknown
Hybrid -x   **Collector-x**
Size: **14" wide**   *Foliage Length:* **6 months**
Hybridizer: **Unknown**   6" pot

photo: Iolanda Marquardt

Neoregelia - 'Sheer Joy'
Hybrid -x   **Collector-x**
Size: **14" wide**   *Foliage Length:* **6 months**
Hybridizer: **Grace Goode**   6" pot

photo: Iolanda Marquardt

Neoregelia - carcharodon variegata
Hybrid -x   *Collector-x*
Size: **24" wide**   *Foliage Length:* **6 months**
Hybridizer: **Chester Skotak**   8" pot

photo: Iolanda Marquardt

Neoregelia - Group of Hybrids
Hybrid -x   *Collector-x*
Size: **14" wide**   *Foliage Length:* **6 months**
Hybridizer: **David Shiigi**   6" pot

photo: Iolanda Marquardt

Neoregelia - 'Painter Delight' variation
Hybrid -x   *Collector-x*
Size: **14" wide**   *Foliage Length:* **6 months**
Hybridizer: **Bill Kirker**   6" pot

photo: Iolanda Marquardt

Neoregelia - fireball Group
Species -x   *Collector-x*   4" pot
Size: **6" wide**   *Foliage Length:* **6 months**

photo: Iolanda Marquardt

Neoregelia - carolinae x compacta
Hybrid -x   **Collector -x**
Size: 14" wide   **Foliage Length:** 6 months
Hybridizer: Chester Skotak   6" pot

photo: Iolanda Marquardt

Neoregelia - 'Van Dorme'
Hybrid -x   **Collector -x**
Size: 14" wide   **Foliage Length:** 6 months
Hybridizer : F. Gruber   6" pot

photo: Iolanda Marquardt

Neoregelia - 'Tri-color Perfecta'
Hybrid -x   **Commercial-x**
Size: 12" wide   **Foliage Length:** 6 months
Hybridizer: Unknown   6" pot

photo: Iolanda Marquardt

Neoregelia - 'Orange Glow'
Hybrid -x   **Collector-x**
Size: 12" wide   **Foliage Length:** 6 months
Hybridizer: Unknown   6" pot

photo: Iolanda Marquardt

Neoregelia - 'Debbie x Cordovan'
Hybrid -x   **Collector -x**
Size: 14" wide   **Foliage Length: 6 months**
Hybridizer: Grant Groves   6" pot

photo: Iolanda Marquardt

Neoregelia - 'Ninja' variation
Hybrid -x   **Collector -x**
Size: 10" wide   **Foliage Length: 6 months**
Hybridizer: David Shiigi   6" pot

photo: Iolanda Marquardt

Neoregelia - 'Kona Gold'
Hybrid -x   **Collector -x**
Size: 14" wide   **Foliage Length: 6 months**
Hybridizer: David Shiigi   6" pot

photo: Iolanda Marquardt

Neoregelia - 'Prince Kuhio' variation
Hybrid -x   **Collector -x**
Size: 14" wide   **Foliage Length: 6 months**
Hybridizer: David Shiigi   6" pot

Neoregelia - 'Carolinae x Kiwi'
Hybrid -x   **Collector-x**
Size: **14" wide**   *Foliage Length:* **6 months**
Hybridizer: **David Shiigi**   6" pot

Neoregelia - 'Kapaa'
Hybrid -x   **Collector-x**
Size: **14" wide**   *Foliage Length:* **6 months**
Hybridizer: **Howard Yamamoto**   6" pot

Neoregelia - Unnamed
Hybrid -x   **Collector-x**
Size: **14" wide**   *Foliage Length:* **6 months**
Hybridizer: **David Shiigi**   6" pot

Neoregelia - 'Manoa Beauty'
Hybrid -x   **Collector-x**
Size: **14" wide**   *Foliage Length:* **6 months**
Hybridizer: **Mike Yamamoto**   6" pot

Neoregelia - concentrica hybrid
Hybrid -x   **Collector-x**
Size: 14" wide   *Foliage Length:* 6 months
Hybridizer: **David Shiigi**   6" pot

Neoregelia - concentrica hybrid
Hybrid -x   **Collector-x**
Size: 14" wide   *Foliage Length:* 6 months
Hybridizer: **David Shiigi**   6" pot

Neoregelia - concentrica hybrid
Hybrid -x   **Collector-x**
Size: 14" wide   *Foliage Length:* 6 months
Hybridizer: **David Shiigi**   6" pot

Neoregelia - concentrica hybrid
Hybrid -x   **Collector-x**
Size: 14" wide   *Foliage Length:* 6 months
Hybridizer: **David Shiigi**   6" pot

Neoregelia - concentrica hybrid
Hybrid -x   **Collecto -x**
Size: 14" wide   **Foliage Length: 6 months**
Hybridizer: **David Shiigi**   6" pot

Neoregelia - 'Dave Fuertes'
Hybrid -x   **Collector-x**
Size: 14" wide   **Foliage Length: 6 months**
Hybridizer: **David Shiigi**   6" pot

Neoregelia - Unnamed
Hybrid -x   **Collector-x**
Size: 14" wide   **Foliage Length: 6 months**
Hybridizer: **David Shiigi**   6" pot

Neoregelia - 'Princess Kaiulani'
Hybrid -x   **Collector-x**
Size: 14" wide   **Foliage Length: 6 months**
Hybridizer: **David Shiigi**   6" pot

photo: Iolanda Marquardt

Neoregelia - 'Kawika'
Hybrid *-x*   **Collector** *-x*
Size: **14" wide**   **Foliage Length: 6 months**
Hybridizer: **David Shiigi**   6" pot

photo: Iolanda Marquardt

Neoregelia - 'Pink Sensation x Grace'
Hybrid *-x*   **Collector** *-x*
Size: **14" wide**   **Foliage Length: 6 months**
Hybridizer: **Grant Groves**   6" pot

photo: Iolanda Marquardt

Neoregelia - 'John Hirota'
Hybrid *-x*   **Collector** *-x*
Size: **14" wide**   **Foliage Length: 6 months**
Hybridizer: **David Shiigi**   6" pot

photo: Iolanda Marquardt

Neoregelia - 'Royal Burgandy'
Hybrid *-x*   **Collector** *-x*
Size: **16" wide**   **Foliage Length: 6 months**
Hybridizer: **Dr. Oeser**   6" pot

Neoregelia - carcharodon albomarginata
Hybrid -x   **Collector -x**
Size: 24" wide   **Foliage Length:** 6 months
Hybridizer: Chester Skotak   8" pot

Neoregelia - 'Grace x Passion'
Hybrid -x   **Collector -x**
Size: 12" wide   **Foliage Length:** 6 months
Hybridizer: Grant Groves   6" pot

Neoregelia - carcharodon variegata
Hybrid -x   **Collector -x**
Size: 24" wide   **Foliage Length:** 6 months
Hybridizer: Chester Skotak   8" pot

Neoregelia - 'Princess Kaiulani'
Hybrid -x   **Collector -x**
Size: 14" wide   **Foliage Length:** 6 months
Hybridizer: David Shiigi   6" pot

photo: Iolanda Marquardt

Neoregelia - 'Sherlette Shiigi'
Hybrid -x   **Collector -x**
Size: **14" wide**   *Foliage Length:* **6 months**
Hybridizer: **David Shiigi**   6" pot

photo: Iolanda Marquardt

Neoregelia - 'Hawaiian Princess'
Hybrid -x   **Collector -x**
Size: **14" wide**   *Foliage Length:* **6 months**
Hybridizer: **David Shiigi**   6" pot

photo: Iolanda Marquardt

Neoregelia - Unnamed
Hybrid -x   **Collector -x**
Size: **14" wide**   *Foliage Length:* **6 months**
Hybridizer: **David Shiigi**   6" pot

photo: Iolanda Marquardt

Neoregelia - carolinae meyendorfii
Hybrid -x   **Collector -x**
Size: **14" wide**   *Foliage Length:* **6 months**
Hybridizer: **BAK**   6" pot

Neoregelia - cacharodon albomarginata
Hybrid -x **Collector -x**
Size:24" wide **Foliage Length: 6 months**
Hybridizer: **Chester Skotak** 8" pot

Neoregelia - cacharodon variegata
Hybrid -x **Collector -x**
Size:24" wide **Foliage Length: 6 months**
Hybridizer: **Unknown** 8" pot

Neoregelia - 'Morado'
Hybrid -x **Collector -x**
Size: 14" wide **Foliage Length: 6 months**
Hybridizer: **Chester Skotak** 6" pot

Neoregelia - 'Cruenta Many Moods'
Hybrid -x **Collector -x**
Size: 14" wide **Foliage Length: 6 months**
Hybridizer: **Unknown** 6" pot

photo: Iolanda Marquardt

Neoregelia - cruenta 'Brazil' variegata
Specie -x   **Collector -x**   6" pot
Size: 14" wide   **Foliage Length: 6 months**

photo: Iolanda Marquardt

Neoregelia - 'Hawaiian Rainforest'
Hybrid -x   **Collector -x**
Size: 14" wide   **Foliage Length: 6 months**
Hybridizer: David Shiigi   6" pot

photo: Iolanda Marquardt

Neoregelia - 'Carolinae x Macwilliamii'
Hybrid -x   **Collector -x**
Size: 14" wide   **Foliage Length: 6 months**
Hybridizer: Chester Skotak   6" pot

photo: Iolanda Marquardt

Neoregelia - 'Passion'
Hybrid -x   **Collector -x**
Size: 18" wide   **Foliage Length: 6 months**
Hybridizer: Grant Groves   6" pot

photo: Iolanda Marquardt

Neoregelia - 'Kahala Dawn' albomarginata
Hybrid -x   ***Collector -x***
Size: **14" wide**   ***Foliage Length:*** **6 months**
Hybridizer: **Bob Okazaki**   6" pot

photo: Iolanda Marquardt

Neoregelia - Unknown
Hybrid -x   ***Collector -x***
Size: **14" wide**   ***Foliage Length:*** **6 months**
Hybridizer: **Unknown**   6" pot

photo: Iolanda Marquardt

Neoregelia - 'Dr. Oeser 100'
Hybrid -x   ***Collector -x***
Size: **14" wide**   ***Foliage Length:*** **6 months**
Hybridizer: **Dr. Oeser**   6" pot

photo: Iolanda Marquardt

Neoregelia - 'Royal Burgandy' variation
Hybrid -x   ***Collector -x***
Size: **16" wide**   ***Foliage Length:*** **6 months**
Hybridizer: **Dr. Oeser**   6" pot

photo: Iolanda Marquardt

Neoregelia - Unnamed
Hybrid -*x*   ***Collector -x***
Size: **14" wide**   ***Foliage Length:*** **6 months**
Hybridizer: **David Shiigi**   6" pot

photo: Iolanda Marquardt

Neoregelia - Unnamed
Hybrid -*x*   ***Collector -x***
Size: **14" wide**   ***Foliage Length:*** **6 months**
Hybridizer: **Sharon Peterson**   6" pot

photo: Iolanda Marquardt

Neoregelia - 'Royal Burgandy' variation
Hybrid -*x*   ***Collector -x***
Size: **16" wide**   ***Foliage Length:*** **6 months**
Hybridizer: **Unknown**   6" pot

photo: Iolanda Marquardt

Neoregelia - Unnamed
Hybrid -*x*   ***Collector -x***
Size: **14" wide**   ***Foliage Length:*** **6 months**
Hybridizer: **David Shiigi**   6" pot

photo: Iolanda Marquardt

Neoregelia - Unnamed
Hybrid -x   **Collector -x**
Size: **1 " wide**   *Foliage Length:* **6 months**
Hybridizer: **David Shiigi**   6" pot

photo: Iolanda Marquardt

Neoregelia - chloristica cv. 'Pink'
Hybrid -x   **Collector -x**
Size: **14" wide**   *Foliage Length:* **6 months**
Hybridizer: **David Shiigi**   6" pot

photo: Iolanda Marquardt

Neoregelia - Unnamed
Hybrid -x   **Collector -x**
Size: **14" wide**   *Foliage Length:* **6 months**
Hybridizer: **David Shiigi**   6" pot

photo: Iolanda Marquardt

Neoregelia - 'Ninja Pink'
Hybrid -x   **Collector -x**
Size: **10" wide**   *Foliage Length:* **6 months**
Hybridizer: **David Shiigi**   6" pot

photo: Iolanda Marquardt

Neoregelia - Unnamed
Hybrid -x   **Collector -x**
Size: 14" wide   **Foliage Length: 6 months**
Hybridizer: **David Shiigi**   6" pot

photo: Ron Parkhurst

Neoregelia - 'Flandria' mutant
Mutant -x   **Collector -x**
Size: 14" wide   **Foliage Length: 6 months**
Owner: **Ron Parkhurst**   6" pot

photo: Christopher Kromrey

Neoregelia - mooreana
Specie -x   **Collector -x**   4" pot
Size: 3" wide   **Foliage Length: 6 months**

photo: Christopher Kromrey

Neoregelia - carolinae 'Painted Lady'
Hybrid -x   **Collector -x**
Size: 14" wide   **Foliage Length: 6 months**
Hybridizer : **Chertser Skotak**   6" pot

photo: Christopher Kromrey

Neoregelia - carolinae 'Imperfecta'
Hybrid -x   **Collector -x**
Size: 14" wide   **Foliage Length:** 6 months
Hybridizer: Chester Skotak   6" pot

photo: Christopher Kromrey

Neoregelia - 'Dawn'
Hybrid -x   **Collector -x**
Size: 14" wide   **Foliage Length:** 6 months
Hybridizer: Unknown   6" pot

photo: Christopher Kromrey

Neoregelia - 'Hawaiian Splash'
Hybrid -x   **Collector -x**
Size: 14" wide   **Foliage Length:** 6 months
Hybridizer: Howard Yamamoto   6" pot

photo: Jacob & Mary Anne Doane-Mau

Neoregelia - 'Grace x Passion'
Hybrid -x   **Collector -x**
Size: 16" wide   **Foliage Length:** 6 months
Hybridizer: Foster/ Groves   6" pot

Neoregelia - 'Dawn'

photo: Christopher Kromrey

Neoregelia - charcharadon albomarginata

photo: Iolanda Marquardt

Vriesea - zamorensis

VRIESEA

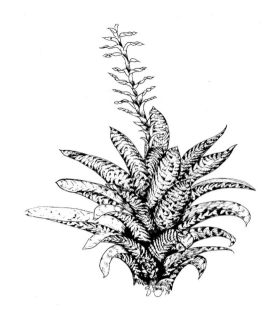

Chapter 10

VRIESEA'S

The Dutch botanist, W. DeVriese, is the person who this family of bromeliads is named after in the 1800's. It has over 200 species and hundreds of hybrids. This family is a good plant for the beginner hybridizer, especially since the plant has an attractive inflorescence.

Again the size difference is vast, ranging from 4 inches in diameter to over 6 feet in diameter. This is one of the few families that are unique in this fashion. Some of the vriesea's are grown for the inflorescence, while others are grown for the foliage. Of course you will see the difference in the following photos. One of the advantages of colorful foliage bromeliads is that they keep their color longer than the inflorescence.

The colors of the inflorescence range from yellows, reds, oranges, pinks, maroons, greens, purples, speckled and combinations. The inflorescence spike is a paddle and sword shape, with some other variations. Whereas the foliage plants have more of a bract inflorescence with no spectacular color.

The foliage is also varied with a wide range of color, markings, bands, stripes and blotches.

Vriesea's are a little harder to grow. One of the general rules is that they like more shade than sun. Of course there are exceptions, such as imperialis, vinicolor, and other similar plants that can tolerate full sun.

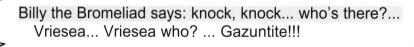

Billy the Bromeliad says: knock, knock... who's there?...
Vriesea... Vriesea who? ... Gazuntite!!!

photo: Iolanda Marquardt

Vriesea - 'Snows of Mauna Kea'
Hybrid -x   **Collector -x**
Size: 18" high   *Foliage Length:* 8 months
Hybridizer: David Shiigi   6" pot

photo: Iolanda Marquardt

Vriesea - 'Favorite'
Hybrid -x   **Commercial -x**
Size: 16" high   *Foliage Length:* 60 days
Hybridizer: Walter Richer   6" pot

photo: Iolanda Marquardt

Vriesea - zamorensis
Species -x   **Commercial -x**   **6" pot**
Size: 16" high   *Foliage Length:* 60 days

photo: Iolanda Marquardt

Vriesea - 'Elan' variegata
Mutant -x   **Collector-x**   **4" pot**
Size: 12" high   *Foliage Length:* 60 days
Owner: Ron Parkhurst

photo: Iolanda Marquardt

Vriesea - glutinosa
Species *-x*   **Collector** *-x*   **8" pot**
Size: 36" high   **Foliage Length:** 90 days

photo: Iolanda Marquardt

Vriesea - ospinae var. guberii
Species *-x*   **Collector** *-x*   **7" pot**
Size: 26" high   **Foliage Length:** 90 days

photo: Iolanda Marquardt

Vriesea - 'Incurvata'
Hybrid *-x*   **Collector** *-x*
Size: 14" high   **Foliage Length:** 60 days
Owner: Ron Parkhurst   **6" pot**

photo: Iolanda Marquardt

Vriesea - 'Tiffany'
Hybrid *-x*   **Commercial** *-c*
Size: 12" high   **Foliage Length:** 60 days
Hybridizer: BAK   **4" pot**

photo: Iolanda Marquardt

Vriesea - 'Poelmanii'
Hybrid -x   **Commercial -x**
Size: 12" high   *Foliage Length:* 60 days
Hybridizer: Duval   6" pot

photo: Iolanda Marquardt

Vriesea - Unnamed
Hybrid -x   **Collector -x**
Size: 12" high   *Foliage Length:* 60 days
Owner: Ron Parkhurst   6" pot

photo: Iolanda Marquardt

Vriesea - 'Madam Pele'
Hybrid -x   **Collector -x**
Size: 30" high   *Foliage Length:* 90 days
Hybridizer: Howard Yamamoto   8" pot

photo: Iolanda Marquardt

Vriesea - tuecherheimii x 'Hawaiian Sunset'
Hybrid -x   **Collector -x**
Size: 48" high   *Foliage Length:* One year +
Hybridizer: David Shiigi   3 gallon pot

photo: Iolanda Marquardt

Vriesea - fosteriana 'White Lighting'
Hybrid -x   **Collector -x**
Size: 24" high   **Foliage Length:** 3 months +
Hybridizer: David Shiigi   8" pot

photo: Iolanda Marquardt

Vriesea - Group of Hybrid
Hybrid -x   **Collector -x**
Size: 24" high   **Foliage Length:** 8 months +
Hybridizer: David Shiigi   8" pot

photo: Iolanda Marquardi

Vriesea - 'Leinaala'
Hybrid-x   **Collector-x**
Size: 24" high   **Foliage Length:** 8 months +
Hybridizer: David Shiigi   8" pot

photo: Iolanda Marquardt

Vriesea - 'Snows of Mauna Kea'
Hybrid-x   **Collector-x**
Size: 24" high   **Foliage Length:** 8 months +
Hybridizer: David Shiigi   8" pot

photo: Iolanda Marquardt

Vriesea - fenestralis x fosteriana 'Selecta'
Hybrid -x   **Collector-x**
Size: 24" high   *Foliage Length:* 8 months +
Hybridizer: David Shiigi   8" pot

photo: Iolanda Marquardt

Vriesea - fenestralis x fosteriana 'Selecta'
Hybrid -x   **Collector -x**
Size: 24" high   *Foliage Length:* 8 months +
Hybridizer: David Shiigi   8" pot

photo: Iolanda Marquardt

Vriesea - 'Empress Michiko'
Hybrid -x   **Collector -x**
Size: 24" high   *Foliage Length:* 8 months +
Hybridizer: David Shiigi   8" pot

photo: Iolanda Marquardt

Vriesea - ''Memorial Howard Yamamoto'
Hybrid -x   **Collector -x**
Size: 24" high   *Foliage Length:* 8 months +
Hybridizer: David Shiigi   8" pot

photo: Iolanda Marquardt

Vriesea - 'Masaml'
Hybrid -x   **Collector -x**
Size: 24" high   **Foliage Length:** 8 months +
Hybridizer: David Shiigi   8" pot

photo: Iolanda Marquardt

Vriesea - fosteriana 'Selecta'
Hybrid -x   **Collector -x**
Size: 24" high   **Foliage Length:** 8 months +
Hybridizer: David Shiigi   8" pot

photo: Iolanda Marquardt

Vriesea - fosteriana cultivar
Hybrid -x   **Collector -x**
Size: 24" high   **Foliage Length:** 8 months +
Hybridizer: David Shiigi   8" pot

photo: Iolanda Marquardt

Vriesea - 'John Hirota'
Hybrid -x   **Collector -x**
Size: 24" high   **Foliage Length:** 8 months +
Hybridizer: David Shiigi   8" pot

Vriesea - 'Howard Yamamoto'
Hybrid -x   **Collector -x**
Size: **24" high**   *Foliage Length:* **8 months +**
Hybridizer: **David Shiigi**   **8" pot**

Vriesea - 'Hawaiian Beauty'
Hybrid -x   **Collector -x**
Size: **24" high**   *Foliage Length:* **8 months +**
Hybridizer: **David Shiigi**   **8" pot**

Vriesea - 'Hawaiian Sunset F2'
Hybrid -x   **Collector -x**
Size: **24" high**   *Foliage Length:* **8 months +**
Hybridizer: **David Shiigi**   **8" pot**

Vriesea - 'Kiku'
Hybrid -x   **Collector -x**
Size: **24" high**   *Foliage Length:* **8 months +**
Hybridizer: **David Shiigi**   **8" pot**

photo: Iolanda Marquardt

Vriesea - Unnamed
Hybrid-x   **Collector-x**
Size: 24" high   **Foliage Length:** 8 months +
Hybridizer: David Shiigi   8" pot

photo: C. Hojo

Vriesea - Group of 'Sherlette'
Hybrid-x   **Collector-x**
Size: 24" high   **Foliage Length:** 8 months +
Hybridizer: David Shiigi   8" pot

photo: Iolanda Marquardt

Vriesea - Unnamed
Hybrid-x   **Collector-x**
Size: 24" high   **Foliage Length:** 8 months +
Hybridizer: David Shiigi   8" pot

photo: Iolanda Marquardt

Vriesea - fosteriana cv 'White Lighting'
Hybrid-x   **Collector-x**
Size: 24" high   **Foliage Length:** 8 months +
Hybridizer: David Shiigi   8" pot

Vriesea - Unnamed
Hybrid-x   **Collector-x**
Size: **24" high**   *Foliage Length:* **8 months +**
Hybridizer: **David Shiigi**   **8" pot**

Vriesea - 'Sherlette'
Hybrid-x   **Collector-x**
Size: **24" high**   *Foliage Length:* **8 months +**
Hybridizer: **David Shiigi**   **8" pot**

Vriesea - heiroglyphica cultivar
Hybrid-x   **Collector-x**
Size: **36" high**   *Foliage Length:* **One year +**
Hybridizer: **David Shiigi**   **2 gallon pot**

Vriesea - Group of Hybrid
                    Collector-x
Size: **24" high**   *Foliage Length:* **8 months +**
Hybridizer: **David Shiigi**   **8" pot**

photo: Iolanda Marquardt

Vriesea - Group of Hybrids
Hybrid-x   **Collector-x**
*Size:*24"high   *Foliage Length:* **8 months +**
Hybridizer: **David Shiigi**   **8" pot**

photo: Iolanda Marquardt

Vriesea - Unnamed
Hybrid-x   **Collector-x**
Size: 24" high   *Foliage Length:* **8 months +**
Hybridizer: **David Shiigi**   **8" pot**

photo: Iolanda Marquardt

Vriesea - Unnamed
Hybrid-x   **Collector-x**
Size: 24" high   *Foliage Length:* **8 months +**
Hybridizer: **David Shiigi**   **8" pot**

photo: Iolanda Marquardt

Vriesea - 'Murakami'
Hybrid-x   **Collector-x**
Size: 24" high   *Foliage Length:* **8 months +**
Hybridizer: **David Shiigi**   **8" pot**

photo: Iolanda Marquardt

Vriesea - 'Mauna Kea' F2
Hybrid-x   **Collector-x**
Size: 24" high   **Foliage Length: 8 months +**
Hybridizer: David Shiigi   8" pot

photo: Iolanda Marquardt

Vriesea - 'Mauna Kea' F2
Hybrid-x   **Collector-x**
Size: 24" high   **Foliage Length: 8 months +**
Hybridizer: David Shiigi   8" pot

photo: Iolanda Marquardt

Vriesea - Unnamed
Hybrid-x   **Collector -x**
Size: 24" high   **Foliage Length: 8 months +**
Hybridizer: David Shiigi   8" pot

photo: Ron Parkhurst

Vriesea - splendens cv. 'Formosa'
Species-x   **Collector-x**   **6" pot**
Size: 14"high   **Flower Length: 60 days**

photo: Iolanda Marquardt

Werauhia - sanguinolenta cv. 'Edna Shiigi'
Hybrid-x   **Collector-x**
Size: *48" high*   **Foliage Length:** one year +
Hybridizer: David Shiigi   3 gallon pot

photo: Iolanda Marquardt

Alcantarea - imperialis cv. 'Black Cinder'
Hybrid-x   **Collector-x**
Size: *48" high*   **Foliage Length:** one year +
Hybridizer: David Shiigi   3 gallon pot

photo: Iolanda Marquardt

Alcantarea - vinicolor
Species-x   **Collector-x**   **2 gallon pot**
Size: *48" high*   **Foliage Length:** one year +

photo: Iolanda Marquardt

Vriesea - Unnamed
Hybrid-x   **Collector-x**
Size: *36" high*   **Foliage Length:** one year +
Hybridizer: David Shiigi   3 gallon pot

photo: Iolanda Marquardt

Vriesea - Unnamed
Hybrid-x   **Collector-x**
Size: 18" high   *Foliage Length:* 8 months +
Hybridizer: David Shiigi   6" pot

photo: Iolanda Marquardt

Vriesea - Unnamed
Hybrid-x   **Collector-x**
Size: 24" high   *Foliage Length:* 8 months +
Hybridizer: David Shiigi   8" pot

photo: Iolanda Marquardt

Vriesea - Unnamed
Hybrid-x   **Collector-x**
Size: 24" high   *Foliage Length:* 8 months +
Hybridizer: David Shiigi   8" pot

photo: Iolanda Marquardt

Vriesea - Unnamed
Hybrid-x   **Collector-x**
Size: 24" high   *Foliage Length:* 8 months +
Hybridizer: David Shiigi   8" pot

photo: Iolanda Marquardt

Vriesea - Unnamed
Hybrid-x   **Collector-x**
Size: **24" high**   *Foliage Length:* **8 months +**
Hybridizer: **David Shiigi**   **8" pot**

photo: Iolanda Marquardt

Vriesea - gigantea seideliana x platynema variegata
Hybrid-x   **Collector-x**
Size: **24" high**   *Foliage Length:* **8 months +**
Hybridizer: **David Shiigi**   **8" pot**

photo: Iolanda Marquardt

Vriesea - 'Hawaiian Sunset'
Hybrid-x   **Collector-x**
Size: **24" high**   *Foliage Length:* **8 months +**
Hybridizer: **David Shiigi**   **8" pot**

photo: Iolanda Marquardt

Vriesea - 'Mauna Kea F2'
Hybrid-x   **Collector-x**
Size: **24" high**   *Foliage Length:* **8 months +**
Hybridizer: **David Shiigi**   **8" pot**

photo: Iolanda Marquardt

Vriesea - 'Tsuro Murakami'
Hybrid-x   **Collector-x**
Size: 30" high   *Foliage Length:* 8 months +
Hybridizer: David Shiigi   2 gallon pot

photo: Iolanda Marquardt

Vriesea - heiroglyphica (interspecie cross)
Hybrid-x   **Collector-x**
Size: 48" high   *Foliage Length:* one year +
Hybridizer: David Shiigi   3 gallon pot

photo: Iolanda Marquardt

Vriesea - 'Maile Lei'
Hybrid-x   **Collector-x**
Size: 30" high   *Foliage Length:* 8 months +
Hybridizer: David Shiigi   2 gallon pot

photo: Iolanda Marquardt

Vriesea - 'Intermedia x fosteriana'
Hybrid-x   **Collector-x**
Size: 24" high   *Foliage Length:* 8 months +
Hybridizer: David Shiigi   8" pot

photo: Iolanda Marquardt

Vriesea - 'Kuulei'
Hybrid-x   **Collector-x**
Size: 36" high   **Foliage Length:** one year +
Hybridizer: David Shiigi   2 gallon pot

photo: Iolanda Marquardt

Vriesea - 'Kuulei'
Hybrid-x   **Collector-x**
Size: 36" high   **Foliage Length:** one year +
Hybridizer: David Shiigi   2 gallon pot

photo: Ron Parkhurst

Vriesea - Unnamed
Hybrid-x   **Collector-x**
Size: 20" high   **Flower Length:** 60 days
ownwer: Ron Parkhurst   6" pot

photo: Iolanda Marquardt

Vriesea - fosteriana 'Red Chestnut F2'
Hybrid-x   **Collector-x**
Size: 24" high   **Foliage Length:** 8 months +
Hybridizer: David Shiigi   8" pot

Vriesea - heiroglyphica x fosteriana 'Red Chestnut F2'
Hybrid -x   **Collector -x**
Size: 48" high   *Foliage Length:* one year +
Hybridizer: David Shiigi 3 gallon pot

Vriesea - Unnamed
Hybrid -x   **Collector -x**
Size: 24" high   *Foliage Length:* 8 months +
Hybridizer: David Shiigi   8" pot

Vriesea - Unnamed
Hybrid-x   **Collector-x**
Size: 20" high   *Foliage Length:* 8 months +
Hybridizer: David Shiigi   6" pot

Vriesea - 'King David Kalakaua'
Hybrid-x   **Collector-x**
Size: 30" high   *Foliage Length:* one year +
Hybridizer: David Shiigi   8" pot

photo: Iolanda Marquardt

Vriesea - Unnamed
Hybrid-x   ***Collector-x***
Size: **30" high**   ***Foliage Length:*** **one year +**
Hybridizer: **David Shiigi   8" pot**

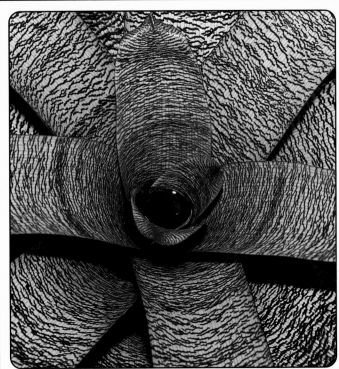

photo: Iolanda Marquardt

Vriesea - 'Kilauea'
Hybrid-x   ***Collector-x***
Size: **30" high**   ***Foliage Length:*** **one year +**
Hybridizer: **David Shiigi   8" pot**

photo: Iolanda Marquardt

Vriesea - Unnamed
Hybrid-x   ***Collector-x***
Size: **30" high**   ***Foliage Length:*** **one year +**
Hybridizer: **David Shiigi   8" pot**

photo: Iolanda Marquardt

Vriesea - Unnamed
Hybrid-x   ***Collector-x***
Size: **30" high**   ***Foliage Length:*** **8 months +**
Hybridizer: **David Shiigi   8" pot**

photo: Iolanda Marquardt

Vriesea - Unnamed

Hybrid-x   **Collector-x**

Size: 30" high   *Foliage Length:* one year +

Hybridizer: David Shiigi   8" pot

photo: Iolanda Marquardt

Vriesea - Unnamed

Hybrid-x   **Collector-x**

Size: 30" high   *Foliage Length:* 8 months +

Hybridizer: David Shiigi   8" pot

photo: Iolanda Marquardt

Vriesea - Unnamed

Hybrid-x   **Collector-x**

Size: 30" high   *Foliage Length:* 8 months +

Hybridizer: David Shiigi   8" pot

photo: Iolanda Marquardt

Vriesea - Unnamed

Hybrid-x   **Collector-x**

Size: 30" high   *Foliage Length:* one year +

Hybridizer: David Shiigi   8" pot

115

photo: Iolanda Marquardt

Vriesea - Unnamed
Hybrid-x   *Collector-x*
Size: 30" high   *Foliage Length:* one year +
Hybridizer: David Shiigi   8" pot

photo: Iolanda Marquardt

Vriesea - Unnamed
Hybrid-x   *Collector-x*
Size: 30" high   *Foliage Length:* one year +
Hybridizer: David Shiigi   8" pot

photo: Iolanda Marquardt

Vriesea - fenestralis
Specie-x   *Collector-x*   8" pot
Size: 30" high   *Foliage Length:* one year +

photo: Iolanda Marquardt

Vriesea - fosteriana 'Red Chestnut F2'
Hybrid-x   *Collector-x*
Size: 30" high   *Foliage Length:* 8 months +
Hybridizer: David Shiigi   8" pot

photo: Iolanda Marquardt

Vriesea - ospinae var. guberii
Specie-x   **Collector-x**   **3 gallon pot**
Size: 48" high   **Foliage Length: one year +**

photo: Iolanda Marquardt

Vriesea - splendens cv. 'Nigra'
Specie-x   **Collector-x**   **6" pot**
Size: 24" high   **Foliage Length: 8 months +**

photo: Iolanda Marquardt

Vriesea - Unnamed
Hybrid-x   **Collector-x**
Size: 20" high   **Foliage Length: 8 months +**
Hybridizer: David Shiigi   **6" pot**

photo: Iolanda Marquardt

Vriesea - Unnamed
Hybrid-x   **Collector-x**
Size: 30" high   **Foliage Length: one year +**
Hybridizer: David Shiigi   **8" pot**

photo: Ron Parkhurst

Vriesea - Purple (unnamed)
Hybrid-x   **Collector-x**
Size: **24" high**   *Foliage Length:* **60 days**
Owner: **Ron Parkhurst**   **6" pot**

photo: Ron Parkhurst

Vriesea - 'Blaze'
Hybrid-x   **Collector-x**   **6" pot**
Size: **16" high**   *Foliage Length:* **60 days**
Hybridizer: **Gonzales**   **Ron Parkhurst Collection**

photo: Ron Parkhurst

Vriesea - Infloresence
Tags mark cross pollination
Hybridizer: **Ron Parkhurst**

photo: Ron Parkhurst

Vriesea - 'Vista'
Hybrid-x   **Collector-x**
Size: **12" high**   *Foliage Length:* **60 days**
Hybridizer: **Kent**   **4" pot**

photo: Ron Parkhurst

Vriesea - heiroglyphica x fosteriana var 'Red Chestnut'
*Owner:*Ron Parkhurst

photo: Ron Parkhurst

Vriesea - heiroglyphica x fosteriana var 'Red Chestnut' variation
*Owner:*Ron Parkhurst

119

Tillandsia - tectorum

TILLANDSIA

Chapter 11

TILLANDSIA'S

Tillandsia's or air plants have the greatest number of species (over 400) and the widest range and variety of any other bromeliad family. They are found as far north as the Mid Atlantic States and way below Brazil. Ranging in size of approx. 1 inch to over 14 feet tall. Tillandsia Usneoides, Spanish Moss or Pele's Hair is one of the most recognized bromeliad (and oldest) other than the pineapple.

This family is unique in many ways. They require little care, but love lots of air movement. Many species will grow on trays without any type of potting mix. They like to be mounted on wood or rocks and some grow in a pot with a mix. One must appreciate the time involved to hybridize or grow Tillandsia's from seed. It is not unusual to have 8 to 10 years go by before you see a mature plant from germination. Some of the plants in my collection are 15 years and older.

One of my favorite Tillandsia is The Tectorum. In many ways it resembles the Silversword plant that grows only on Mount Haleakala on the island of Maui, Hawaii. If there were no oceans in the world, Mount Haleakala would be the third largest mountain in the world. Number one and two largest mountains would be on the Big Island of Hawaii, where it has snow part of the year. I held the ski record for a number of years.

Billy the bromeliad says: What do you call a farmer who plows his field next to an ocean with the first letter of the alphabet? Till-land-sea-a!

photo: Iolanda Marquardt

Tillandsia - wagneriana
Species-x   *Collector-x*   **6" pot**
Size: **12" high**   *Flower Length:* **3 months**

photo: Iolanda Marquardt

Tillandsia - dyeriana
Specie-x   *Collector-x*   **4" pot**
Size: **12" high**   *Flower Length:* **2 months**

photo: Iolanda Marquardt

Tillandsia - tectorum
Specie-x   *Collector-x*   **Bare Root**
Size: **6" high**   *Flower Length:* **9 months+**

photo: Iolanda Marquardt

Tillandsia - rothii
Specie-x   *Collector-x*   **Bare Root**
Size: **16" high**   *Foliage Length:* **3 months**

photo: Iolanda Marquardt

Tillandsia - tectorum
Species-x   **Collector-x**   **Bare Root**
Size: 6" high   ***Foliage Length:*** 9 months+

photo: Iolanda Marquardt

Tillandsia - ehlersiana
Specie-x   **Collector-x**   **Bare Root**
Size: 3" high   ***Foliage Length:*** 2 weeks

photo: Iolanda Marquardt

Tillandsia - funckiana
Specie-x   **Collector-x**   **Bare Root**
Size: 6"high   ***Foliage Length:*** - 2 weeks

photo: Iolanda Marquardt

Tillandsia - roland gosselinii
Spices-x   **Collector-x**   **Bare Root**
Size: 16" high   ***Foliage Length:*** 3 months

123

photo: Iolanda Marquardt

Tillandsia - bulbosa
Species -x   Collector -x   Bare Root
Size: 6" high   Foliage Length: 12 months

photo: Iolanda Marquardt

Tillandsia - Unnamed
Hybrid -x   Collector -x
Size: 6" high   Foliage Length: 12 months
Owner: Ron Parkhurst   4" pot

photo: Iolanda Marquardt

Tillandsia - stricta
Specie-x   Collector-x   Bare Root
Size: 5" high   Flowere Length: 2 weeks

photo: Iolanda Marquardt

Tillandsia - juncea
Specie-x   Collector-x   Bare Root
Size: 12" high   Flower Length: 1 month

Tillandsia - edithae
Species-x   **Collector-x**   **Bare Root**
Size: **6" high**   *Flower Length:* **3 weeks**

photo: Iolanda Marquardt

Tillandsia - caput medusae
Specie-x   **Collector-x**   **Bare Root**
Size: **8" high**   *Flower Length:* **2 months**

photo: Iolanda Marquardt

Tillandsia - ionantha
Specie-x   **Collector-x**   **Bare Root**
Size: **3" high**   *Flower Length:* **2 weeks**

photo: Iolanda Marquardt

Tillandsia - stricta
Specie-x   **Collector-x**   **Bare Root**
Size: **4" high**   *Foliage Length:* **2 weeks**

125

photo: Iolanda Marquardt

Tillandsia - queroensis and tricolor
Species -x   **Collector -x   Bare Root**
Size:10" high   **Foliage Length: 3 months**

photo: Iolanda Marquardt

Tillandsia - jalisco monticola
Specie -x   **Collector-x Bare Root**
Size: 10" high   **Flower Length: 3 months**

photo: Iolanda Marquardt

Tillandsia - cyanea
Specie-x   **Collector-x   4"pot**
Size: 8" high   **Foliage Length: 1 month**

photo: Iolanda Marquardt

Tillandsia - Assorted Tillandsia
Specie-x   **Collector-x   Bare Root**

photo: Iolanda Marquardt

Tillandsia - funckiana and stricta
Species-x   **Collector-x**
Size: 8" high   ***Flower Length:*** 3 months

photo: Iolanda Marquardt

Tillandsia - filifolia
Specie-x   **Collector-x Bare Root**
Size: 12" high   ***Flower Length:*** 2 months

photo: Iolanda Marquardt

Tillandsia - usneoides or 'Spanish Moss'
Speci -x   **Collector-x Bare Root**
Size: 14" long   ***Flower Length:*** 12 months

photo: Iolanda Marquardt

Tillandsia - Unknown
Specie-x   **Collector-x Bare Root**
Size: 8" high   ***Foliage Length:*** 12 months

photo: Iolanda Marquardt

Tillandsia - cyanea 'Anita'
Hybrid-x   **Collector-x**
Size: 8" high   ***Foliage Length:*** 12 months
Hybridizer: Unknown   4" pot

photo: Iolanda Marquardt

Tillandsia - rothii
Specie-x   **Collector-x**   **Bare Root**
Size: 16" high   ***Flower Length:*** 3 months

photo: Iolanda Marquardt

Tillandsia - ehlersiana
Species-x   **Collector-x**   **Bare Root**
Size: 8" high   ***Foliage Length:*** 12 months

photo: Iolanda Marquardt

Tillandsia - duratii
Specie-x   **Collector-x**   **Bare Root**
Size: 24" long   ***Foliage Length:*** 12 months

Tillandsia - ionantha
Specie-x   **Collector-x**   **Bare Root**
Size: 3" high   **Flower Length:** 2 weeks

photo: Iolanda Marquardt

Tillandsia - stricta
Specie-x   **Collector-x**   **Bare Root**
Size: 6" high   **Flower Length:** 2 weeks

photo: Iolanda Marquardt

Tillandsia - stricta x ionantha
Hybrid-x   **Collector-x**   **Bare Root**
Size: 3" high   **Foliage Length:** 12 months
Hybridizer: **Dimmitt**

photo: Iolanda Marquardt

Tillandsia - zecheri
Specie-x   **Collector-x**   **Bare Root**
Size: 6" high   **Foliage Length:** 12 months

Tillandsia - matudae
Specie-x   **Collector-x**   **Bare Root**
Size: 12" high   **Flower Length:** 2 months

Tillandsia - chiapensis c.s. gardner
Specie-x   **Collector-x**   **Bare Root**
Size: 8" high   **Foliage Length:** 12 months

Tillandsia - polystachia
Specie-x   **Collector-x**   **Bare Root**
Size: 5" high   **Foliage Length:** 1 month

Tillandsia - chiapensis
Specie-x   **Collector-x**   **Bare Root**
Size: 16" high   **Flower Length:** 2 months

Tillandsia - lepidosepala

photo: Iolanda Marquardt

Specie-x   ***Collector-x***   **Bare Root**
Size: **6" high**   ***Flower Length:*** **12 months**

photo: Iolanda Marquardt

Tillandsia - Assorted

Specie-x   ***Collector-x***   **Bare Root**
Size: **4" high**   ***Foliage Length:*** **12 months**

photo: Iolanda Marquardt

Tillandsia - didisticha

Specie-x   ***Collector-x***   **Bare Root**
Size: **10" high**   ***Flower Length:*** **3 months**

photo: Iolanda Marquardt

Tillandsia - kammit

Specie-x   ***Collector-x***   **Bare Root**
Size: **4" high**   ***Foliage Length:*** **12 months**

photo: Iolanda Marquardt

Tillandsia - brachycaulos
Specie-x   **Collector-x**   **Bare Root**
Size: **10" high**   *Flower Length:* **2 months**

photo: Iolanda Marquardt

Tillandsia - didisticha
Specie-x   **Collector-x**   **Bare Root**
Size: **12" high**   *Flower Length:* **2 months**

photo: Iolanda Marquardt

Tillandsia - ' Feather Duster'
Hybrid-x   **Collector-x**   **Bare Root**
Size: **12" high**   *Foliage Length:* **12 months**
Hybridizer: **Dimmit**

photo: Iolanda Marquardt

Tillandsia - brachycaulos
Specie-x   **Collector-x**   **Bare Root**
Size: **8" high**   *Foliage Length:* **1 month**

Tillandsia - dyeriana

Specie-x   **Collector-x** 4" pot
Size: 12" high   *Foliage Length:* 3 weeks

photo: Iolanda Marquardt

Tillandsia - jalisco monticola

Specie-x   **Collector-x**   **Bare Root**
Size: 14" high   *Flower Length:* 2 months

photo: Iolanda Marquardt

Tillandsia - flabellata

Hybrid-x   **Collector-x**   4" pot
Size: 6" high   *Foliage Length:* 12 months

photo: Iolanda Marquardt

Tillandsia - Assorted

Hybrid-x   **Collector-x**   **Bare Root**
Size: 12" high   *Foliage Length:* 12 months
Owner: Ron Parkhurst

photo: Ron Parkhurst

photo: Christopher Kromrey

Tillandsia - rothii
Species-x   **Collector-x**   **Bare Root**
Size: 14" high   *Flower Length:* **2 months**

photo: Christopher Kromrey

Tillandsia - funckiana
Specie-x   **Collector-x**   **Bare Root**
Size: 6" high   *Foliage Length:* **12 months**

photo: Iolanda Marquardt

Tillandsia - lorentziana
Specie-x   **Collector -x**   **Bare Root**
Size: 10" high   *Flower Length:* **2 months**

photo: Iolanda Marquardt

Tillandsia - cyanea 'Anita'
Hybrid-x   **Collector -x**
Size: 8" high   *Foliage Length:* **2 months**
Hybridizer: **Unknown**   **4" pot**

S. Shiugi '98

Bigeneric Guzmania x Vriesea

THE OTHER BROMELIAD FAMILIES

illustration by: Jim Frey

Chapter 12

I do not have time and the space to go into detail with the other bromeliad families. There are very many interesting bromeliads in this category. Commercially at this point, very few growers venture into the "other" families on a large scale. I find many attractive inflorences, shapes and foliage design in many of these species and hybrids. I also believe we are just at the tip of the iceberg with the bromeliad industry and the possibilities are great with this diverse family. Cut flowers, landscape and interiorscaping to name a few. In any event, a picture is worth a thousand words and this is what this chapter is about, to give you a broader overview of some of the "other" families.

Maui Pineapple, the best eating bromeliad in the world! Our friends at Maui Pineapple Company have been growing pineapple for over 100 years! With over 9,000 acres planted in pineapple, Maui Pineapple Company is still the only company in the United States continuing to can pineapple. Whether it is fresh whole pineapple, canned pineapple or vacuum packed fresh pineapple, insist on "100% Hawaiian"(tm) grown pineapple. Taste the difference!

Bromeliaceae Family

Bromeliodeae:
1. Acanthostachys
2. Aechmea
3. Ananas
4. Androlepis
5. Araeococcus
6. Billbergia
7. Bromelia
8. Canistrum
9. Cryptanthus
10. Deinacanthon
11. Disteganthus
12. Fascicularia
13. Fernseea
14. Greigia
15. Hohenbergia
16. Hohenbergiopsis
17. Lymania
18. Neoglaziovia
19. Neoregelia

Bromeliodeae:
20. Nidularium
21. Ochagavia
22. Orthophytum
23. Portea
24. Pseudaechmea
25. Pseudananas
26. Quesnelia
27. Ronnbergia
28. Streptocalyx
29. Wittrockia

Pitcairnioideae:
30. Abromeitiella
31. Ayensua
32. Brewcaria
33. Brocchinia
34. Connellia
35. Cottendorfia
36. Deuterocohnia
37. Dyckia
38. Encholirium
39. Fosterella
40. Hectia
41. Lindmania
42. Navia
43. Pepinia
44. Pltcairnia
45. Puya
46. Steyerbromelia

Tillandsidioideae:
47. Catopsis
48. Glomeropitcairnia
49. Guzmania
50. Mezobromelia
51. Tillandsia
52. Vriesea
   a. Werauhia
   b. Alcanteria

photo: Iolanda Marquardt

Nidularium - rutilans
Species-x   **Collector-x**   **6"pot**
Size: 20" high   *Foliage Length:* **90 days +**

photo: Iolanda Marquardt

Nidularium - begeloides
Species-x   **Collector-x**   **6"pot**
Size: 20" high   *Foliage Length:* **60 days +**

photo: Iolanda Marquardt

Orthophytum - gurkenii
Species-x   **Collector-x**   **6"pot**
Size: 16" high   *Foliage Length:* **90 days +**

photo: Iolanda Marquardt

X-Neophytum - 'Gary Hendrix'
Hybrid-x   **Collector-x**
Size: 20" high   *Foliage Length:* **120 days +**
Hybridizer: Nat Deleon   **6"pot**

photo: Iolanda Marquardt

Portea - petropolitana var. extensa
Species-x   **Collector-x**   **3 gallon pot**
Size: 48" high   **Foliage Length: 90 days +**

photo: Iolanda Marquardt

Portea - Unnamed
Hybrid-x   **Collector-x**
Size: 36" high   **Foliage Length: 90 days +**
Owner: **Ron Parkhurst**   **2 gallon pot**

photo: Iolanda Marquardt

Portea - neotigii
Species-x   **Collector-x**   **2 gallon pot**
Size:36" high   **Foliage Length: 60 days +**

photo: Iolanda Marquardt

Anana's - 'Ivory Coast' albomarginata
Hybrid-x   **Collector-x**
Size: 24" high   **Foliage Length: 90 days +**
Hybridizer: Unknown   **8" pot**

139

photo: Iolanda Marquardt

Ananas - comosus 'Pineapple'
Species-x   **Collector-x   8" pot**
Size: 30" high   **Foliage Length:** 30 days +

photo: Iolanda Marquardt

Nidularium - billbergioides var. citrinum
Species-x   **Collector-x   6" pot**
Size: 20" high   **Foliage Length:** 60 days +

photo: Iolanda Marquardt

Orthophytum - saxicolo
Specie-x   **Collector-x   6" pot**
Size: 16" high   **Foliage Length:** 60 days +

photo: Iolanda Marquardt

'X-Neophytum - 'Firecracker'
Hybrid-x   **Collector-x**
Size: 12" high   **Foliage Length:** 90 days +
Hybridizer: Gary Hendrix   6" pot

photo: Iolanda Marquardt

'X-Neophytum - 'Ralph Davis'
Hybrid-x   ***Collector-x***
Size: **20" high**   ***Foliage Length:*** **90 days +**
Hybridizer: **Nat Deleon   6" pot**

photo: Iolanda Marquardt

'X-Neophytum - 'Gary Hendrix'
Hybrid-x   ***Collector-x***
Size: **18" high**   ***Foliage Length:*** **90 days +**
Hybridizer: **Nat Deleon   6" pot**

photo: Iolanda Marquardt

Intergeneric - Vriesea / Guzmania
Hybrid-x   ***Collector-x***
Size: **30" high**   ***Foliage Length:*** **90 days +**
Owner: **Ron Parkhurst   7" pot**

photo: Iolanda Marquardt

Ananas - nanus
Specie-x   ***Collector-x***   **4" pot**
Size: **16" high**   ***Foliage Length:*** **90 days +**

photo: Iolanda Marquardi

Hoenbergia - stellata
Species-x   ***Collector-x***   **2 gallon pot**
Size: **36" high**   ***Flower Length:*** **90 days +**

photo: Iolanda Marquardi

Nidularium - regeloides cv. 'Leperosa'
Hybrid-x   ***Collector-x***
Size: **12" high**   ***Foliage Length:*** **90 days +**
Hybridizer: **Bob Cole**   **6" pot**

photo: Iolanda Marquardi

Dyckia - fosteriana
Species-x   ***Collector-x***   **6" pot**
Size: **8" high**   ***Foliage Length:*** **6 months +**

photo: Iolanda Marquardi

Dyckia - platyphylla
Species-x   ***Collector-x***   **4" pot**
Size: **6" high**   ***Foliage Length:*** **90 days +**

Dyckia - Unknown
Specie-x   **Collector-x   4" pot**
Size: **6" high**   *Foliage Length:* **60 days +**

'X-Neophytum   - 'Gallactic Warrior'
Hybrid-x   **Collector-x**
Size: **12" high**   *Foliage Length:* **3 mouths**
Hybridizer: **Antle   6" pot**

Quesnelia - aruensis
Specie-x   **Collector-x   2 gallon pot**
Size: **30" high**   *Foliage Length:* **30 days +**

Neophytum - 'Firecracker'
Hybrid-x   **Collector-x**
Size: **12" high**   *Foliage Length:* **90 days +**
Hybridizer: **Gray Hendrix   6" pot**

143

Alii Lei   Designer: Ron Parkhurst   photo: Randy Hufford

144

CUT FLOWERS AND LIVE FLORAL ARRANGEMENTS

Chapter 13

When we first were getting started in the bromeliad business, I had an idea of placing bromeliads in an attractive basket. I was told it would never work. Not only did it work, but also it kept us alive in our early years. We have since come to use bromeliads in hand made baskets, ceramic pots, rocks and driftwood media's. The trick with live basket arrangements is to use a plastic liner and top off the basket with green moss. We also use a cinder rock as a topping off finish or decorative rock. We do this also with the ceramic pot arrangements.

photo: Christopher Krumrey

World Bromelisd Conference - Houston

Large pots, planters and areas where there are more then a dozen plants, we first prep the site with a loose material, such as cinders or wood bark. At this point you might want to bury empty pots bigger then the ones you are using in the design you have planned. With rocks and driftwood mounts, we will use green moss around where plants have been mounted. A low heat glue gun is recommended.

Why live floral arrangements? Beside the visual aspect, they last a long time! You get your monies worth. You'll pay $20.00 on up for an arrangement, but it will last a month or two!

Next, I want to talk a little about cut flowers. This is a very new and exciting area. How many flower arrangements have you seen with cut bromeliad flowers in them? In fact, if you take all of the florist shops in the world, many of them would not know what a bromeliad is! Other's have heard of bromeliads, but do not know where to get cut bromeliad flowers on a commercial level. I would venture to say that less than 5% have used cut bromeliad flowers and most of them not on a regular basis. What is the reason? One reason is that we are only at the tip of the iceberg of the bromeliad industry. Another reason is the time invested to get a single flower, usually takes about two years. After that much time, the grower will want to get the most money for his plant. That is why you will see more potted bromeliads, verses cut bromeliad flowers. Therefore, cut bromeliad flowers will be one of the most expensive flowers in the world! On the other hand, cut bromeliad flowers is one of the longest lasting cut flowers in the industry. One the average cut bromeliads will last 2 to 3 weeks, I have had some last 4, 5 and 6 weeks! Beside their lasting value, the added bonus of shapes, colors and varieties make bromeliads the number one choice.

Billy the bromeliad says: Bromeliad arrangements are good for any occasion. Surprise someone!

Guzmania 'Puna Gold' In Baskets
Designer. Ron Parkhurst

Assorted Cuts
Hanalei Nursery

Assorted Cut Bromeliads in the shape of Maui
Representing the 75th Maui County Fair
Designer. Ron Parkhurst

Tillandsia dyeriana in Basket
Designer. Patrice Parkhurst

Cut Guzmania 'Rana' :
Hanalei Nursery

photo: Iolanda Marquardt

photo: Iolanda Marquardt

Aechmea gamosepala in a Basket
Designer : Patrice Parkhurst

photo: Iolanda Marquardt

Guzmania 'Puna Gold' in a Basket
Designer : Ron Parkhurst

photo: Iolanda Marquardt

Cut Guzmania 'Puna Gold'
and 'Kapoho Flame'
Glenn Matsubara Bromeliad Cut Flowers

photo: Randy Hufford

Alii Lei with Guzmania 'Puna Gold' and
'Kapoho Flame' Designer: Ron Parkhurst

photo: Iolanda Marquardt

Assorted Guzmania's in a Large Basket
Designer: Ron Parkhurst

photo: Iolanda Marquardt

Cut Guzmania 'Puna Gold':
Hanalei Nursery

photo: Iolanda Marquardt

Cut Guzmania lingulata:
Hanalei Nursery

149

Assorted Guzmania in a Large Basket
Designer: Ron Parkhurst

Assorted Cut Bromeliads in a Vase
Designer: Ron Parkhurst

Bromeliad Arrangement
Designer: Janet Brown

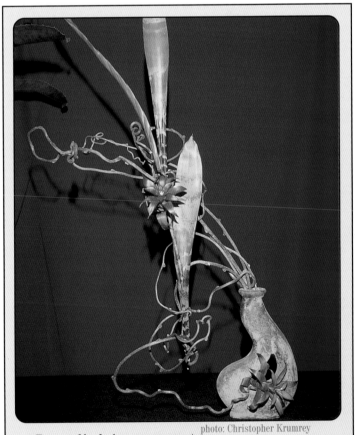

Bromeliad Arrangement
Designer: Michael Young

Bromeliad Arrangement
Designer: Janet Brown

photo: Christopher Krumrey

Bromeliad Arrangement
Designer: Unknown

photo: Christopher Krumrey

Bromeliad Arrangement
Designer: Unknown

photo: Christopher Krumrey

Bromeliad Arrangement
Designer: Unknown

photo: Christopher Krumrey

Bromeliad Arrangement
Designer: Unknown

photo: Christopher Krumrey

Bromeliad Arrangement
Designer: Unknown

photo: Christopher Krumrey

Bromeliad Arrangement
Designer: Abbie Owen

photo: Christopher Krumrey

Bromeliad Arrangement
Designer: Unknown

photo: Christopher Krumrey

Bromeliad Arrangement
Designer: Unknown

photo: Christopher Krumrey

Bromeliad Arrangement
Designer: Unknown

photo: Christopher Krumrey

Bromeliad Arrangement
Designer: Unknown

photo: Christopher Krumrey

Bromeliad Arrangement
Designer: Unknown

photo: Christopher Krumrey

Bromeliad Arrangement
Designer: Unknown

photo: Christopher Krumrey

Bromeliad Arrangement
Designer: Unknown

photo: Christopher Krumrey

Bromeliad Arrangement
Designer: Lou Trahan

photo: Christopher Krumrey

Bromeliad Arrangement
Designer: Inge Whitman

photo: Christopher Krumrey

154

Bromeliad Arrangement
Designer: Lon Trahan

photo: Christopher Krumrey

Bromeliad Arrangement
Designer: Ron Parkhurst

photo: Waterson Photography

Bromeliad Arrangement
Designer: Ron Parkhurst

photo: Waterson Photography

Bromeliad Arrangement
Designer: Ron Parkhurst

photo: Waterson Photography

Bromeliad Arrangement
Designer. Ron Parkhurst

Bromeliad Arrangement
Designer: Ron Parkhurst

Bromeliad Tree at Hotel Hana Resort (808-248-8211)

Cynbidiums and Bromeliads

LANDSCAPING AND INTERIORSCAPING

Chapter 14

This is where most of the bromeliads are used. It is where the accent of a bromeliad design is highlighted. The core of the industry.

How did bromeliads become so popular with indoor settings? Variety, lasting blooms, foliage and shapes are some of the reasons. Bromeliads will accent any of your garden designs or will make excellent gardens by themselves.

To use bromeliads in large pots, planters, waterfalls and areas where more then 6 bromeliads are used, we do the following. First we make sure that the borders are in place and ready for plants. Next, make sure the area where you are going to put the bromeliads is loose, such as cinders or wood bark. If the area you are working in will be "changed out" with more bromeliads when they have expired, we recommend that you bury a slightly larger pot in the planting area flush with the surface. Example, most bromeliads are grown in 6" pots, so put a 7" empty pot just below your planter surface and the top of the 7" pot flush with your surface. That way, you can place the live bromeliad in a 6" pot in the 7" permanent placed pot for easy removal and installation.

Of course a pre-designed plan is helpful and your change out will go a lot easier. Always keep your bromeliads in their growing pots for the best results. When bromeliads are in an enclosed area, over watering can be a problem. A moisture meter found at your local hardware store will be most helpful. Let the bromeliads dry out in their cups and pots before watering. Misting the inflorescence and leaves prolongs your plants life.

Landscaping with bromeliads is also very easily done. We offer the following tips. Plan your area of design before you start. You might want to include some main features in your garden such as a waterfall, pond, rocks and driftwood. Some larger plants for shade is also recommended such as tree ferns, various small palms, and other mid-side plants. For the shadier areas you will want Guzmania's and Vriesea's. For the sunny areas you might want Neoregelia's and other sun tolerant bromeliads. Again, you want to dig out an area where the pot goes to fit in the hole, then have a top dress over the dirt. To enhance the colors of your bromeliads, mist with water or use a leaf shine obtained from your local florists. Mounting bromeliads in trees and rocks also add to your garden appeal. Use your imagination and creativity!

Billy the bromeliad says: What do you call a jailbird who flies the coop? An Interiorscape!

photo: Iolanda Marquardt

B o s s a   N o v a

photo: Iolanda Marquardt

Interiorscape:
Aechmea 'Eileen' in Planter Pot

photo: Iolanda Marquardt

Interiorscape:
Assorted Guzmania in Planter Pot

photo: Iolanda Marquardt

Interiorscape:
Guzmania 'Corrine' in a Large Planter

photo: Iolanda Marquardt

Interiorscape:
Assorted Bromeliads and Orchids in a Planter Pot

161

photo: Iolanda Marquardt

Interiorscape:
Aechmea-'Friederike' in Planter Box

photo: Iolanda Marquardt

Interiorscape:
Guzmania-' Rana' in Planter Box

photo: Iolanda Marquardt

Interiorscape:
Guzmania 'Rana' and squarosa in Planter

photo: Iolanda Marquardt

Interiorscape: Assorted Bromeliads from
Hanalei Nursery at a Trade Show

162

photo: Iolanda Marquardt

Interiorscape:
Assorted Bromeliads in Large Planter

photo: Iolanda Marquardt

Interiorscape:
Assorted Bromeliads in Planter

photo: Iolanda Marquardt

Interiorscape:
Assorted Guzmania's with Waterfall

photo: Ron Parkhurst

Interiorscape:
Guzmania - Assorted Herb Hill Hybrids

photo: Iolanda Marquardt

Interiorscape:
Assorted Bromeliads in a Large Planter

photo: Iolanda Marquardt

Interiorscape:
Assorted Bromeliads in Large Planter

photo: Iolanda Marquardt

Interiorscape:
Bromeliads in a Tree Planter

photo: Iolanda Marquardt

Interiorscape:
Bromeliads in a Tree Planter

164

Interiorscape:
Assorted Bromeliads in a Large Planter

photo: Iolanda Marquardt

Interiorscape:
Guzmania-'Puna Gold'

photo: Iolanda Marquardt

photo: Iolanda Marquardt

Interiorscape: Cynbidium Orchids and
Bromeliads in a Large Planter

photo: Iolanda Marquardt

Interiorscape: Cynbidium Orchids and
Bromeliads in a Large Planter

Interiorscape:
Guzmania-'Rana' in a Planter Box

Interiorscape:
Assorted Bromeliads in a Large Planter

Landscape:
Assorted Neoregelia's

Landscape:
Neoregelia-compacta

166

photo: Iolanda Marquardt

Landscape:
Aechmea Blanchetiana Neoregla Royal Burgandy

photo: Iolanda Marquardt

Landscape:
Assorted Neoregelia's

photo: Iolanda Marquardt

Landscape:
Aechmea Blanchetiana Assorted Neoregelia's

photo: Iolanda Marquardt

Landscape:
Neoregelia-'Macwilliamsii'

167

Landscape:
Assorted Bromeliads

Landscape:
Neoregelia Hybrids-David Shiigi

Landscape:
Neoregelia Hybrids-David Shiigi

Landscape:
Aechmea-fasciata

photo: Iolanda Marquardt

Landscape:
Neoregelia-'Bossa Nova'

photo: Iolanda Marquardt

Landscape:
Vriesea-imperialis Hybrid

photo: Iolanda Marquardt

Landscape:
Vriesea-heiroglyphica

photo: Iolanda Marquardt

Landscape:
Aechmea-blanchetiana

photo: Iolanda Marquardt

Landscape:
Assorted Bromeliads

photo: Iolanda Marquardt

Landscape:
Assorted Bromeliads

photo: Iolanda Marquardt

Landscape:
Assorted Bromeliads

photo: Iolanda Marquardt

Landscape:
Guzmania-'Cherry' in a Planter

Landscape:
Assorted Bromeliads

Landscape:
Neoregelia-'Grace x Passion' in a Planter

Landscape:
Aechmea-fasciata & Tillandsia-Cyanea'

Landscape:
Assorted Bromeliads

171

photo: Iolanda Marquardt

Landscape:
Assorted Neoregelia

photo: Iolanda Marquardt

Landscape:
Assorted Guzmania

photo: Iolanda Marquardt

Landscape:
Aechmea-'Eileen'

photo: Iolanda Marquardt

Landscape:
Guzmania - 'Kapoho Fire' (unauthorized
plants in tissue culture)

172

photo: Iolanda Marquardt

Landscape:
Vriesea-'Favorite'

photo: Iolanda Marquardt

Landscape:
Assorted Bromeliads

photo: Iolanda Marquardt

Landscape:
Assorted Bromeliads

photo: Iolanda Marquardt

Landscape:
Assorted Bromeliads

Landscape:
Bonsai Tree in Pot by: David Fukumoto

Landscape:
Bonsai Tree in Pot by: David Fukumoto

Landscape:
Bonsai Rock and Plant by: David Fukumoto

Landscape:
Bonsai Rock and Plant by: David Fukumoto

Bromeliad Show in Houston

World Bromeliad Show

Torch Ginger

ORCHIDS AND OTHER TROPICALS

Chapter 15

Living in Hawaii, lush tropical beauty is an everyday part of life.
This is why I wanted to add this chapter in the book. It has
nothing to do with bromeliads, just God's beautiful creation.
While tropical flowers are used in landscape, interiorscape and
cut flowers, I will not go into culture or care of these plants. It will
strictly be a visual pleasure. So enjoy!

Billy the bromeliad says's:
I love orchids and
tropicals too!

Tahitian Ginger

photo: Iolanda Marquardt

177

Torch Ginger

Protea-'Pink Mink '

Heliconia-'Caribaea Purpurea'

Heliconia-'Rostrata'

Bird of Paradise

Orange Trump Vine

Thumbergia Mysorensis

Thumbergia Grandiflora

photo: Iolanda Marquardt

Protea-'Pincushion'

photo: Iolanda Marquardt

Plumeria-'Pink Red'

photo: Iolanda Marquardt

Plumeria-'Yellow'

photo: Iolanda Marquardt

Rubber Vine

photo: Iolanda Marquardt

Red Alamanda

photo: Iolanda Marquardt

Water Lily

photo: Iolanda Marquardt

Passion Fruit Flower

photo: Iolanda Marquardt

Protea - 'King'

photo: Iolanda Marquardt

Plumeria - 'Pink'

photo: Iolanda Marquardt

Water Lily

photo: Iolanda Marquardt

Spectable Ginger (Honeycomb)

photo: Iolanda Marquardt

Tahitian Ginger

Tahitian Ginger

Heliconia - 'Sexy Pink'

Haleakala Silversword

Haleakala Silversword in Bloom

photo: Iolanda Marquardt

Heliconia - 'Sexy Pink'

Red Ginger

photo: Iolanda Marquardt

photo: Iolanda Marquardt

Water Hyacinth

photo: Iolanda Marquardt

Heliconia - 'Caribaea Purpurea'

photo: Iolanda Marquardt

Protea - 'Pink Mink'

photo: Iolanda Marquardt

Protea - 'Pink Mink'

photo: Iolanda Marquardt

Blue Ginger

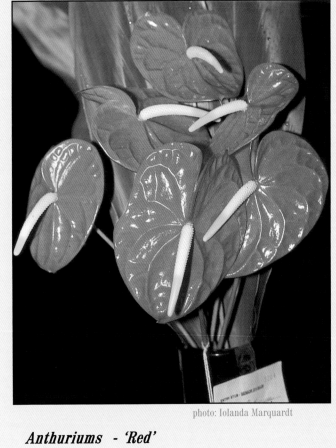

photo: Iolanda Marquardt

Anthuriums - 'Red'

Bird of Paradise

Heliconia - 'Citicorum'

Water Lily

Prickly Pear

Heliconia - 'Citicorum'

Heliconia - 'Pagoda'

Shell Ginger

Yellow Bush Allamanda

photo: Iolanda Marquardt

Yellow Hibiscus

photo: Iolanda Marquardt

Heliconia - 'Xanthobillosa'

photo: Iolanda Marquardt

Morning Glory

photo: Iolanda Marquardt

Canna Lily

photo: Iolanda Marquardt

Protea - 'King'

photo: Iolanda Marquardt

Protea - 'Orange Frost'

photo: Iolanda Marquardt

Football Vine

photo: Iolanda Marquardt

Rose Mammow

189

photo: Ron Parkhurst

Oil Painting by: F.L.Parkhurst

Elizabeth Parkhurst

photo: Iolanda Marquardt

Amaranthus

photo: Iolanda Marquardt

Ornamental Banana

photo: Iolanda Marquardt

Green Jade Vine

photo: Iolanda Marquardt

Red Hibiscus

photo: Iolanda Marquardt

Red Plumeria

photo: Iolanda Marquardt

Brazilian Plume

photo: Iolanda Marquardt

Ohia Lehua

photo: Iolanda Marquardt

Amaranthus

photo: Iolanda Marquardt

Purple Bougainvillea

photo: Iolanda Marquardt

Hawaiian Hibiscus - Yellow

192

photo: Iolanda Marquardt

White Ginger

photo: Iolanda Marquardt

Pink Fruit Banana

photo: Iolanda Marquardt

Canna Lily

photo: Iolanda Marquardt

Cup of Gold

193

photo: Iolanda Marquardt

Amaranthus

photo: Iolanda Marquardt

Orchid   'Sun Fun Beauty'

photo: Iolanda Marquardt

Orchid - Miltonidiun

photo: Iolanda Marquardt

Orchid   Dendrobium - 'Candy Stripe'

Orchid Alicera - 'Flying High'

Orchid Cattleya - 'Bryce Kanion'

Orchid Paphiopedilum 'Maudii'

Orchid Cattleya 'Faye Miyamoto'

photo: Iolanda Marquardt

Orchid Cattleya

photo: Iolanda Marquardt

Orchid Miltumnopsis

photo: Iolanda Marquardt

Orchid Ascocenda - 'Yip Sum Wah'

photo: Iolanda Marquardt

Orchid Brassidium - 'Tacoma Ridge'

photo: Iolanda Marquardt

Orchid Brassidium

photo: Iolanda Marquardt

Orchid Cattleya Gutatta

photo: Iolanda Marquardt

Orchid Cattleya-'Casidas Spring'

photo: Iolanda Marquardt

Wiliwili

197

Orchid Colmonara-'Wild Cat'

Orchid 'Orange Beauty'

Orchid Dendrobium - 'Waianae Blush'

Orchid Vanda

198

Orchid Phalaenopsis-'Happy Valentine'

Orchid Phalaenopsis-'Kathleen Ai'

Orchid Cattleye-'Fred Stuart'

Orchid Cynbidium

Orchid Dendrobium -'Lahaina Stripe'

Orchid Dendrobium -'Bangkok Fancy Galaxy'

Orchid Dendrobium

Orchid Phalaenopsis

Orchid   Cattleya - 'Princess Bells'

Orchid   Vanda - 'Purple'

Orchid   Cattleya - 'Bow Bells'

Magnolia

Orchid Phalaenopsis

photo: Iolanda Marquardt

photo: Iolanda Marquardt

Protea - 'Pink Mink'

Bromeliad Tree Designed by:
 Ron Parkhurst & Immanuel Angel Rennaissance Wailea

PRODUCTS AND SERVICES

Chapter 16

Besides giving general information about bromeliads, this book will be your reference and catalog when ordering bromeliads, products and services. It is a coffee table book and a catalog for all your needs. For better service the contents of this chapter, we have set up a Home Page for this section. This section will be updated regularly. Our homepage is www.maui.net/~hanalei/flowers/ Direct all responses to hanalei@maui.net or Hanalei Nursery, P.O.Box 827, Makawao, Hawaii 96768 USA. Comments/ suggestions welcomed. "Check our website, see you there! www.maui.net/~hanalei/flowers/

1. Hanalei Nursery - story

2. Photography by Iolanda Marquardt/ Flavio Alves Assistant Photographer
   - custom prints, calenders and cards from photo's within this book.

3. Oil paintings and prints -custom oil painting reproductions by F. L. Parkhurst
   and ink drawings by Sherlette Shiigi from this book.

4. Tee-shirts - 'Maui Style' tm, Hawaiiana T-Shirts by R. W. Parkhurst / F. L. Parkhurst

5. Cut flower mix - prolongs the shelf life of cut flowers.

6. Pots/ mix/ fertilizer/ tools - pre-packaged mix with pots and fertilizer, ready to plant.

7. Maui Marriott Hotel - a beautiful landscaped resorts on Kaanapali Beach
   for reservations call 1-808-667-1200

8. Embassy Suites Maui / Kaanapali Beach Hotel - Resorts on Maui with Bromeliads
   for reservations call 1-808-661-2000 / 1-808-661-0011

9. Greenhouses and supplies - packaged models to fit your designs.

10. Bromeliad wine and champagne - pineapple blanc and pineapple champagne.
    shipped by two's.

11. Maui pineapple - fresh, canned or vacuum packed.

12. Plant orders - bromeliads, bromeliads and more bromeliads.
    see our webpage for selection and prices.

13. Baskets - custom hand made baskets.

14. Rocks/ driftwood - for mounting bromeliads.

15. Florists supplies - bamboo vases, moss, props.

16. Hawaiian Airlines - pacific and west coast. Cargo and travel. Call 1-808-871-6132

17. Aquaponics tm - self contain units to raise fish and organic vegetables.

18. Calenders and Greeting Cards - from "The Book of Bromeliads" photographers.

19. Wood Bowls and Boxes - custom Hawaiian bowls and boxes.

20. Rock Pots - use for 4", 6" and gallon pots.

Iolanda Marquardt Photography

Iolanda Marquardt is a Maui-based photographer who does work in a variety of subfields, including nature and special event photography, portraits, and photojournalism. She is a mamber of the Professional Photographers of Hawai'i, and her photographs have won top honors in recent statewide competitions.

Marquardt graduated with a degree in Journalism from the University of Vale do Rio, in Rio Grande do Sul, Brazil. In 1986, she began working as a reporter and photojournalist for the daily newspaper *Correio do Povo*. Her early photographs documented events of local and national importance, including the Brazilian expedition to Antarctica in 1988.

After she came to the United States in 1991, Marquardt became more involved in photographing nature, and she completed courses in nature photography at Harper College in Chicago. Since 1995, she has lived and worked in Hawai'i, where she has been able to study under Richard A. Cooke III, a former photographer for *National Geographic* and an auther of photography books.

Marquardt's most recent awards include a first place in the 1998 Allen-Tarleton Statewide Competition, for her slide essay on "Celebrating the Hana Taro Fest." In the same year, she earned second place for her black and white photography in the "state open" category at the Maui County Fair. Two of her photographs depicting aspects of local culture were chosen to be in the 1999 Maui County Calender, in an open competition, At the 1997 Maui County Fair, Marquardt placed second in the "Maui open" slide contest.

Iolanda Marquardt

Mike Segura - Landscape Director
Maui Marriott Resort

BROMELIAD SPECIE FOUND ON MAUI!!

Extra, extra, read all about it! New bromeliad species found on the top of Haleakala, Maui, Hawaii. This bromeliad is found no where else in the world! The species is in the Tillandsia family and named Silversword, because of it's silver, sword like blades. Mature plants take up to 20 years to bloom, with a spectacular 3-foot infloresence!

Tillandsia Silversword

photo: Ron Parkhurst

Note: WARNING: The author has been known to pull practical jokes. All information deemed reliable, but not guaranteed!

CLOSING

Chapter 16

There is something that sparks the soul when one sees fresh flowers and unusual plants. It's medicinal to our very being. It makes us feel good during bad and good times. It is a reminder of our creator and this gives us hope.

Our goal is to cause a spark and interest in bromeliads; the rest is up to you! Start a collection, make your own arrangements or start a nursery! Whether you are already growing bromeliads, a beginner, or a consumer, these are my favorite plants that will inspire your life. Thank you! (Mahalo Nui Loa and Aloha Ke Akua!)

Other Bromeliad books to read:
1) Blooming Bromeliads by Baensch
2) Tillandsia's by Isley III
3) Growing Bromeliads by Bromeliad Society of Australia
4) The Colorful Bromeliads by Padilla
5) Tillandsia Handbook by Shimizu + Takizawa
6) Canistropsis by Leme

22   Christopher Krumrey

Christopher Krumrey, 39, A native Texan, professional photographer, BSI accredited judge since May 1996, cultivating bromeliads since the early 1980's.

Active member of the Bromeliad Society International, Bromeliad Society of Austin, Bromeliad Society of Houston, and The Southwest Bromeliad Guild.

Attended world conferences in Tampa, Fl, 1992, San Diego, Ca., 1994,(awards photographer), and Orlando, F1., 1996, (awards photographer for the Judges Certification Committee), and Houston, TX. 1998 (awards photographer).

Backpacking expeditions throughout the South and Southwestern United States as adult advisor for the Boy Scouts of America has led to an extensive collection of landscape and wildflower photography.

Interests include the pond culture of Japanese Koi and the culture of bromeliads, orchids, begonias, and tropical plants.

Greenhouse, gardens and collections featured on PBS KLUR television program Central Texas Gardener, Sept. 1991 and March 1997.

Max Sabas
Landscape Director
Embassy Suites Resort

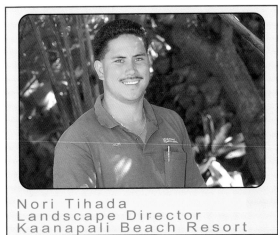

Nori Tihada
Landscape Director
Kaanapali Beach Resort

glossary

Acantha – thorn

Acute leaf – tapering to a point

Adventitous-sprout – pup, keiki, or offspring

Albomarginata – white on the margin of the leaves and green down the center

Ampule – bottle shape

Angiosperm – plant with seeds in a sac

Anther – pollen sacs

Anthesis – flower open and ready for pollen

Anthocyanin – pigments that causes color in bromeliads

Apex - at the tip or top of the plant

Apical meristem – part of the root or adventitious sprout from which a tissue culture lab can reproduce identical plants from the mother plant

Asexual – sexless plant

Atmospheric – plants that get nutrients from the air

Axil – where leaf and stem meet

Axis – the main stem of a plant

Banded – crossmarks on leaves

Basal – the area at the base of the plant

Basitonal – pups, offsets or keiki's that grows from the base of the mother plant

Bicolor – two colors

Bigeneric – the cross between two plants of a different genera in the same plant family

Blade – section of leaf, including the tip

Bract – a colored leaf on the inflorescence

Calyx – a protective covering in the flower parts

Capsule – a seed pod

Chlorophyll – green pigment in plants

Clone – plants reproduced in a lab from a mother plant, with the same characteristics

Crown – the point where the roots start from the main plant

Cultivar – a plant that is different from the other plants grown from seed

Deciduous – the loss of leaves

Discolor – the loss of color in the inflorescence or leaves

Ecology – relationships between organisms and the environment

Endemic – native plants in a specific geographical area

Environment – a natural habitat or man made

Epidermal – protective covering of a plant part

Epiphyte – a plant that grows on another plant or object, but does not feed on it

F1 – first generation of a hybrid

F2 – second generation of self-fertilized plants from F1 plants

Fenestralis – light green rectangular areas on a leaf, such as Vriesea Fenestralis

Fertile – producing pollen and seeds

Foliar – leaves or plant foliage

Foliage – leaves of a plant

Fungicide – chemical that kills fungi

Genus – related plants in a group of plants

Germination – the sprouting of a seed

Grex – a group of species or hybrids plants from a seed pod

Habitat – geographical area where a plant grows naturally

Heterogeneous – different or varying

Hybrid – the crossing of two different plants

Indigenous – native to an area, not introduced

Inflorescence – the part that holds the individual flowers, bracts, and floral head

Keiki – Hawaiian for small, pup, or offspring

Leaf – the foliage part of a plant

Lepidote – covered with small scales

Meristem – the area which produces new leaf or offshoots

Monocarp – flowers only once

Mutant – a plant that differs from the mother plant

Nematodes – microscopic worms that attack the root and base structure of a plant

Node – a point at the base of a leaf where an offshoot could form

Nutrient – food substance needed for growth

Obtuse Leaf – rounded or blunt at the end

Offset – a small plant from the mother that forms at the base

Orthotropic – growing towards the light

Ph – chemical symbol to determine the soil analysis. 7.0 being neutral, above being alkaline, below being acidic

Pathogen – a desease producing organism

Perennial – plants that survive a whole years season or more

Petal – a leaf of the flower

Photosynthesis – the process by which plants uses the sun's light to convert carbon dioxide to oxygen. Note: plants also absorb toxins out of the air

Pistal – female part of the flower

Pollen – male part of the flower

Polystichous – leaves formed in a circular fashion around the base of a plant

Propagule – a plant from seed or from an offshoot from the mother plant that is growing on its own

Quilling – the rolling of the center leaves, sometimes for lack of water in the cup

Rainforest – a natural habitat in a jungle where many bromeliads and other epiphytes are found

Rhizome – a root that travels underground and sends up shoots, that in turn grows as a single plant

Rosette – a circular arrangement of flowers found in the cup of the Neoregelia family

Saphrophyte – bromeliads or other plants in their natural habitat that obtain food by decaying organic matter

Saxicolous – bromeliads that grow on rocks

Scale – a pest that attaches to the leaves of bromeliads

Scape – the stem of the inflorescence

Self-fertilization – producing seed from the same plant

Sepal – the flower parts covering the petals

Species – a group of plants, which have similar characteristics, yet is different from other groups

Sphagnum moss – used as a media for some orchids and terrestrial bromeliads or as a base for mounting plants

Spike – the rising of the inflorescence, but still not to maturity

Sport - a bromeliad that differs in characteristic from the mother plant

Stamen – the pollen appendage of the flower

Stigma – long stem that forms a new plant, in turn, forms a new plant, etc

Succulent – a plant that stores water in its leaves, stem, base, and/or roots

Systematics – the study of plants and their characteristics among plants

Taxonomy – the classification and order of plants

Terrestrial – grows in the ground

Trichome – the scale or pore like function that absorbs moisture and nutrients through the leaves

Type – specimen or species that has been named

Variegation - white down the center of leaves and green on the margins

Variety – a slight difference from a specimen

Vegetative Reproduction – by offshoots of the mother plant

Viability – seeds that will germinate

Virus – a microscopic disease

Wetting agent – soap like material used with potting mix for water distribution

Xerophyte – drought resistant plants, such as bromeliads

Zink – a soft metal ore, sometimes associated with the name David, sometimes unpredictable, definitely not a bromeliad.

index

Maui Flower Growers Association
1-800-805-2758
www.mauiflower.com

213

Jacob and Mary Anne Doane-Mau possibly have the largest library of Hawaiian tropical flower, foliage and native plants in the world. Their works consist of Original Photographs, Lithographs and Iris Gicle printed on canvas. Jacob has been published in several books including Maui On My Mind, Proteas in Hawaii and Exotic Tropicals of Hawaii. They have done several calendars, a wide-range of notecards, postcards, brochures, a view book, a floral identification poster, and sell their prints that are beautifully matted and framed under the Lahaina Banyan Tree every weekend.

Their work is recognized and used by Biologists and Artists alike, who appreciate their attention to detail and color quality.

For more information about their work, please contact them at e-mail; flowersphotos@juna.com or, www.hawaiiflowerphotosetc.com or fax; (808) 871-7060

215

Anthurium 'Midori
Hawaii's Prreiere
Anthurium Hybridizer: Calvin Hayashi